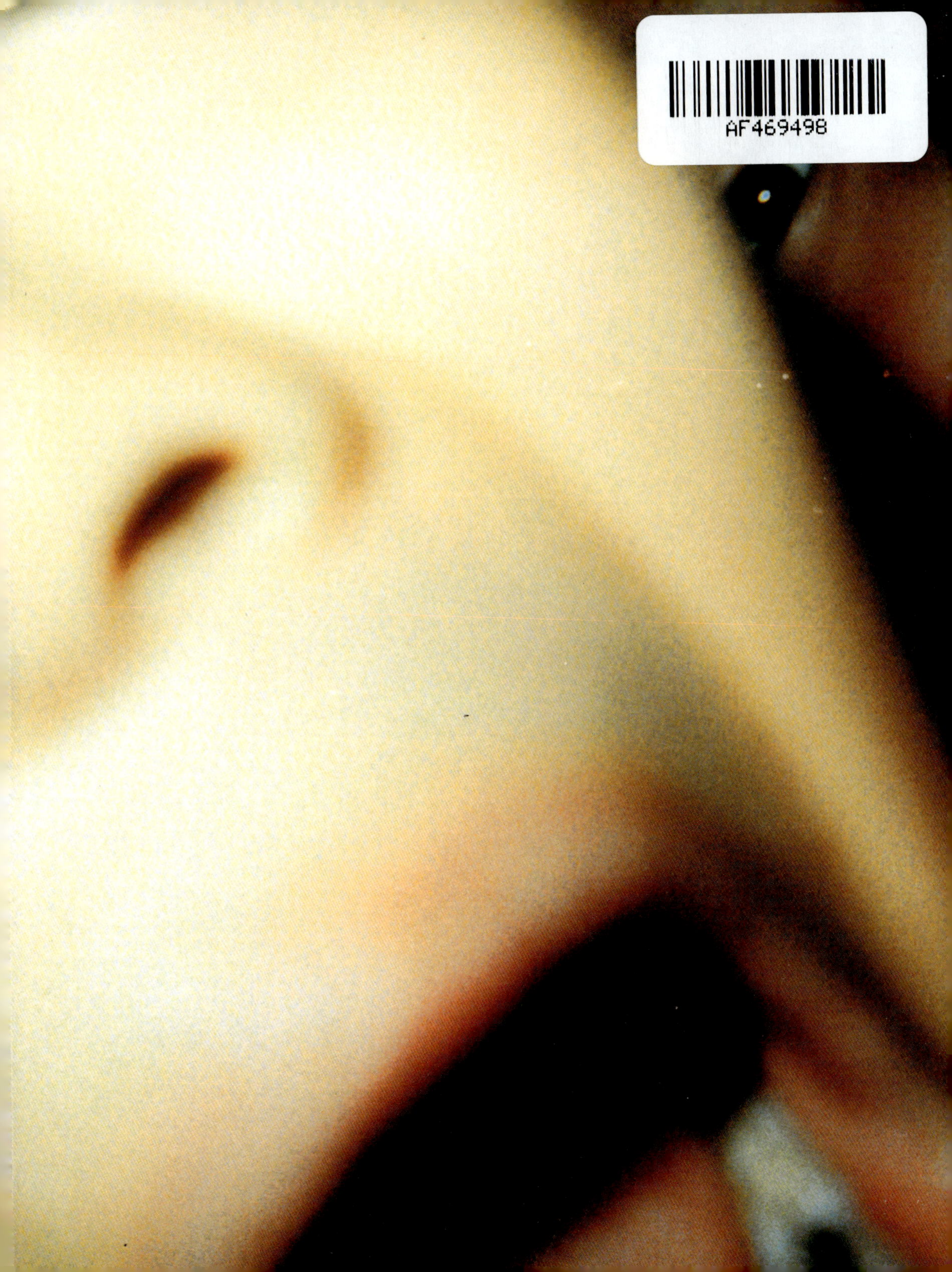
AF469498

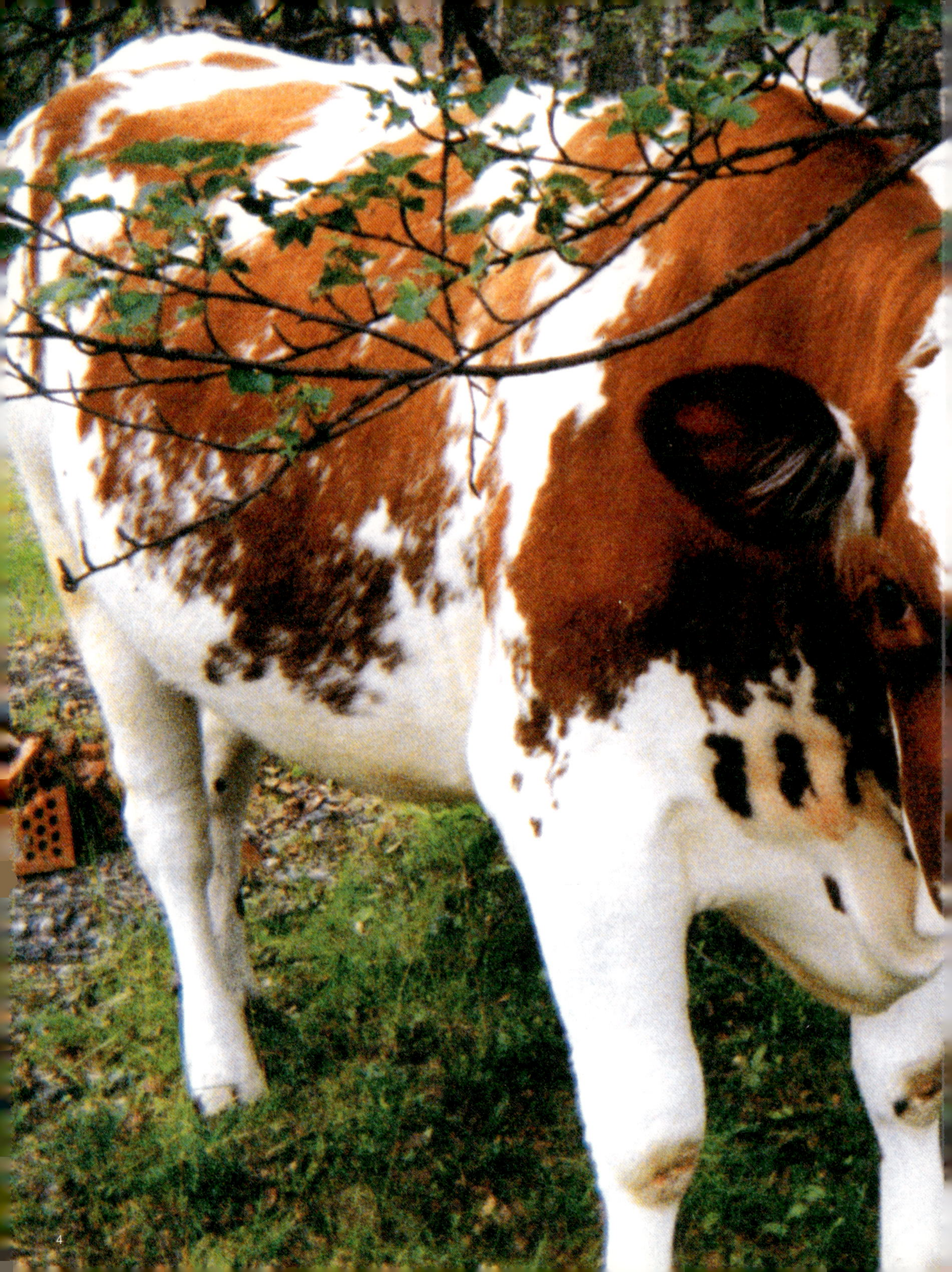

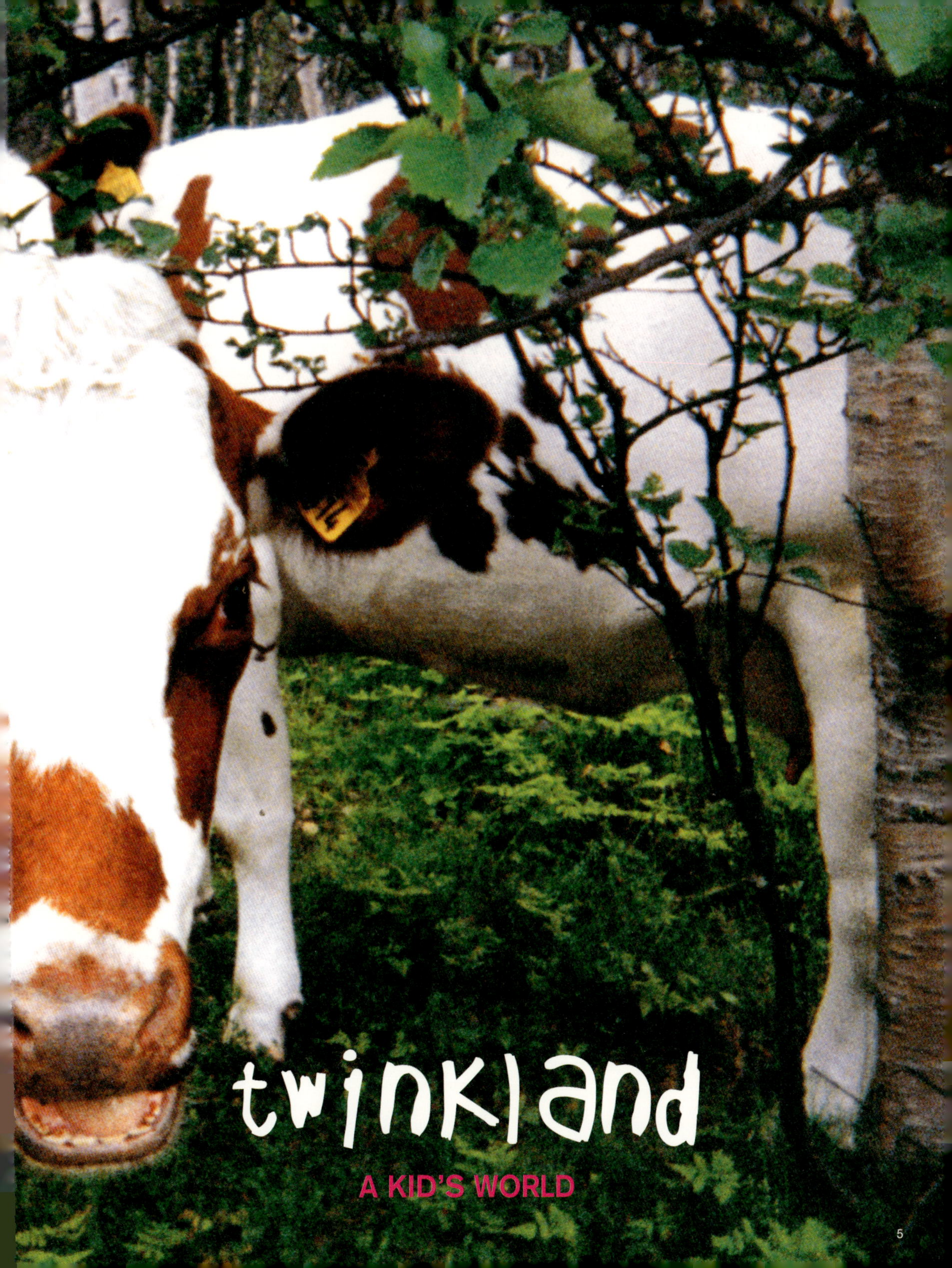
twinkland
A KID'S WORLD

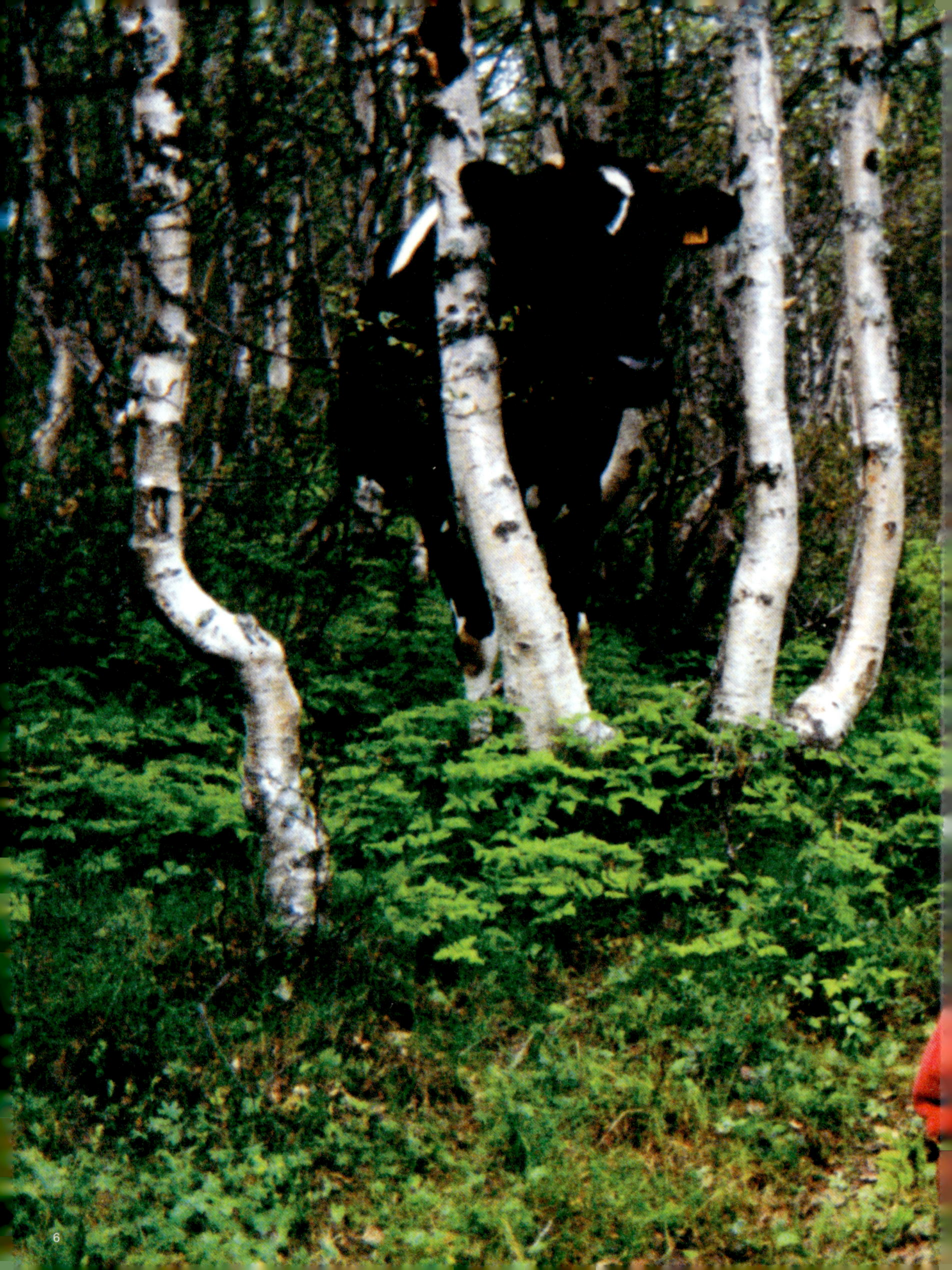

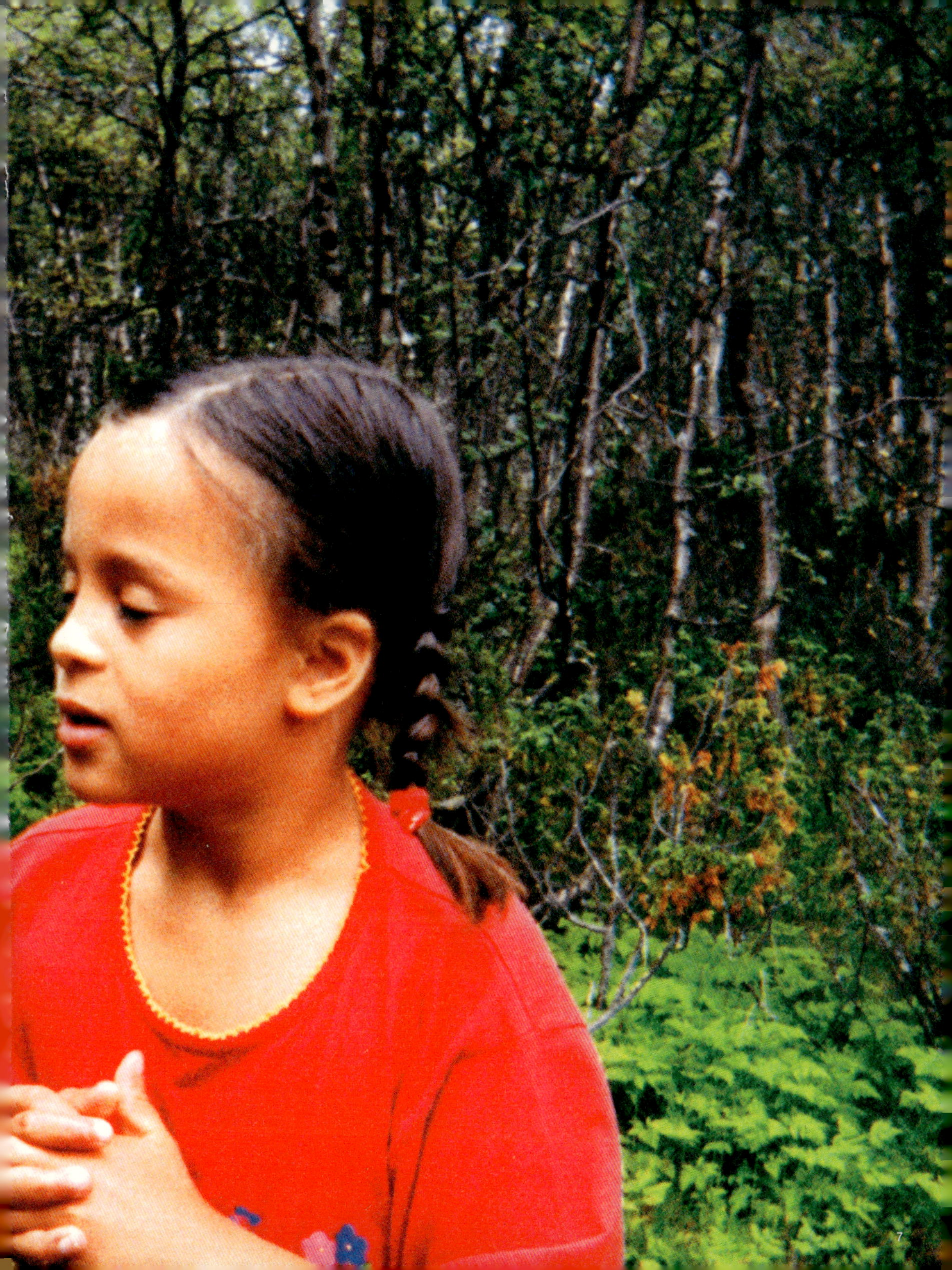

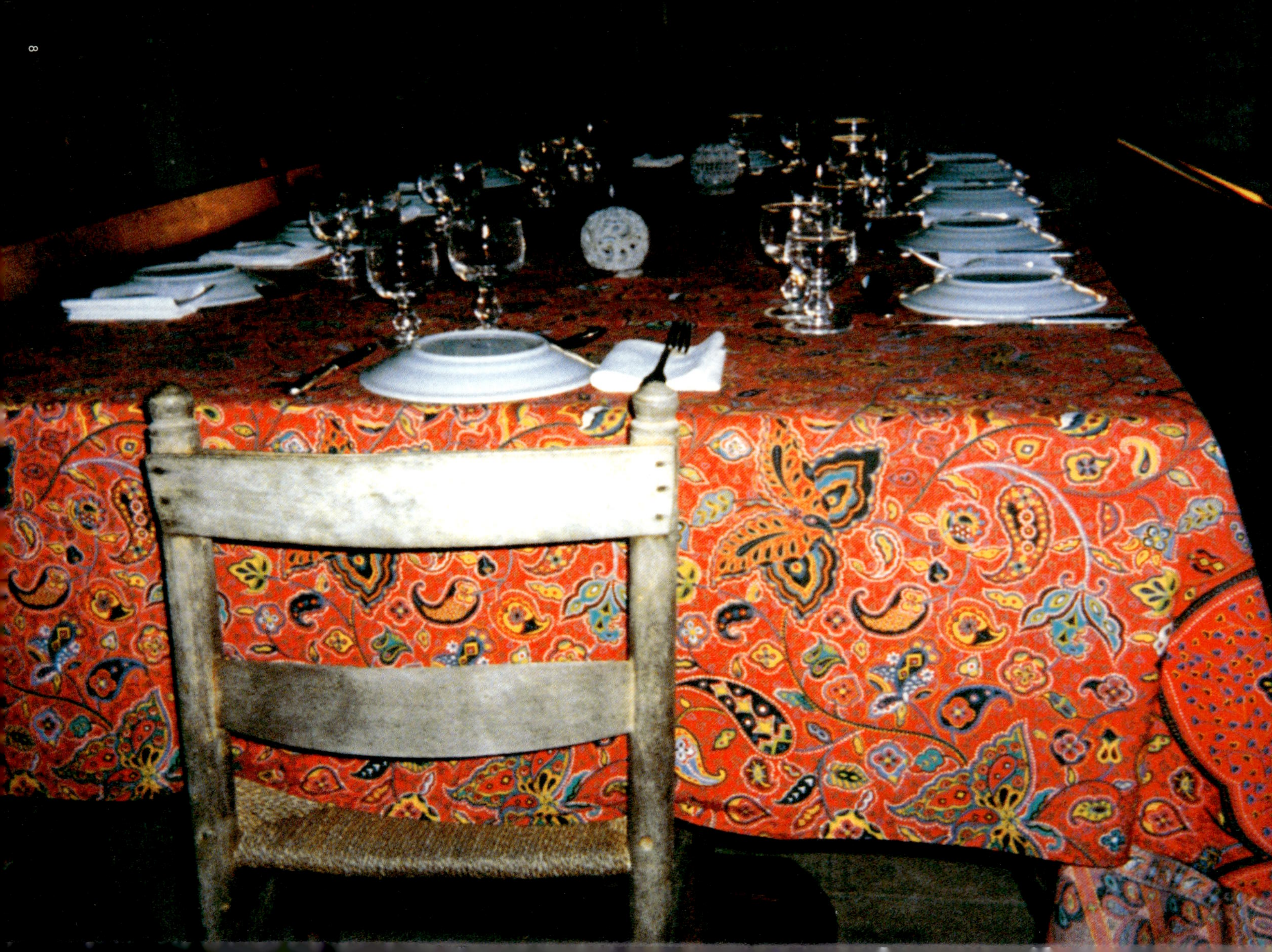

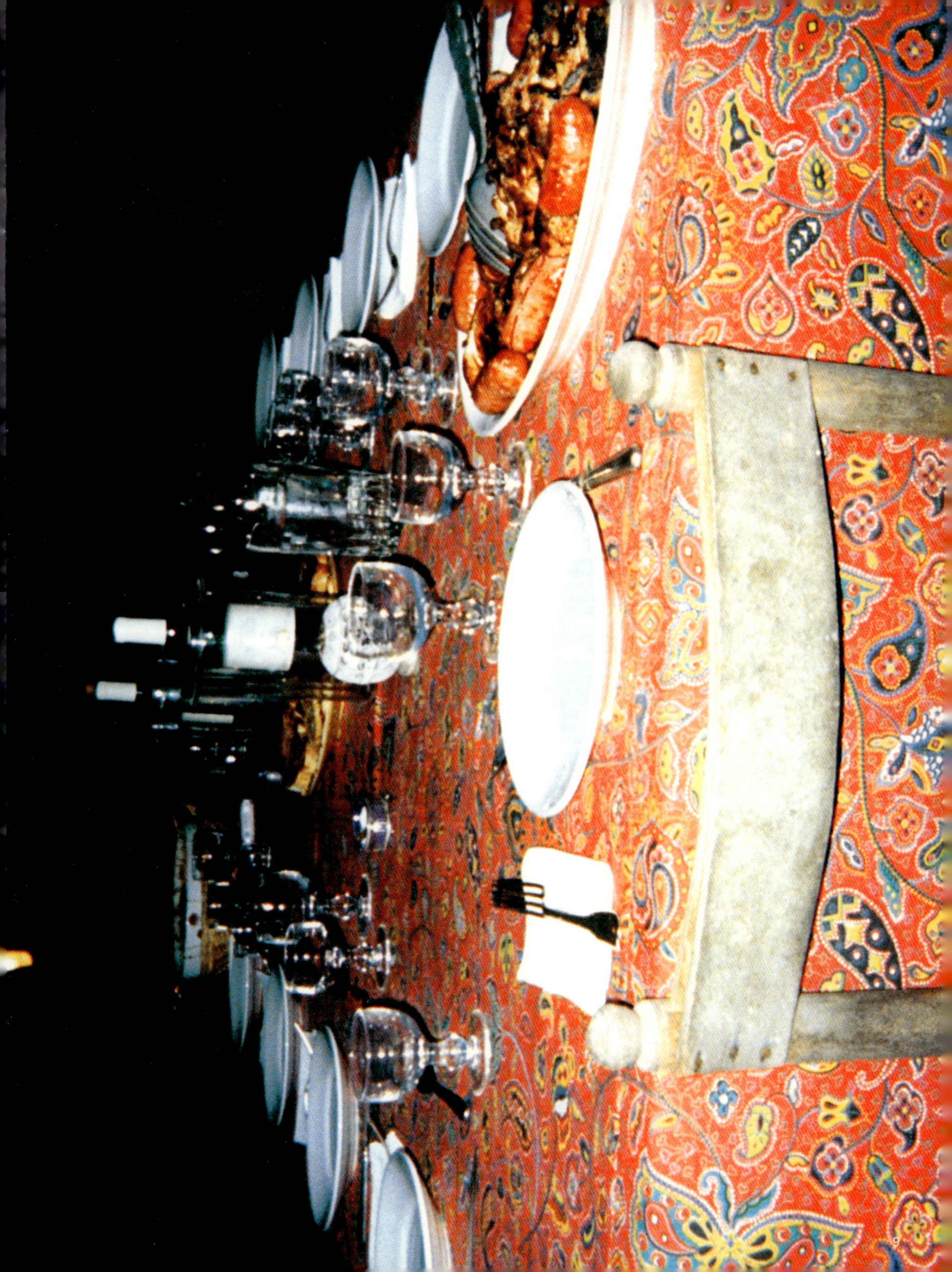

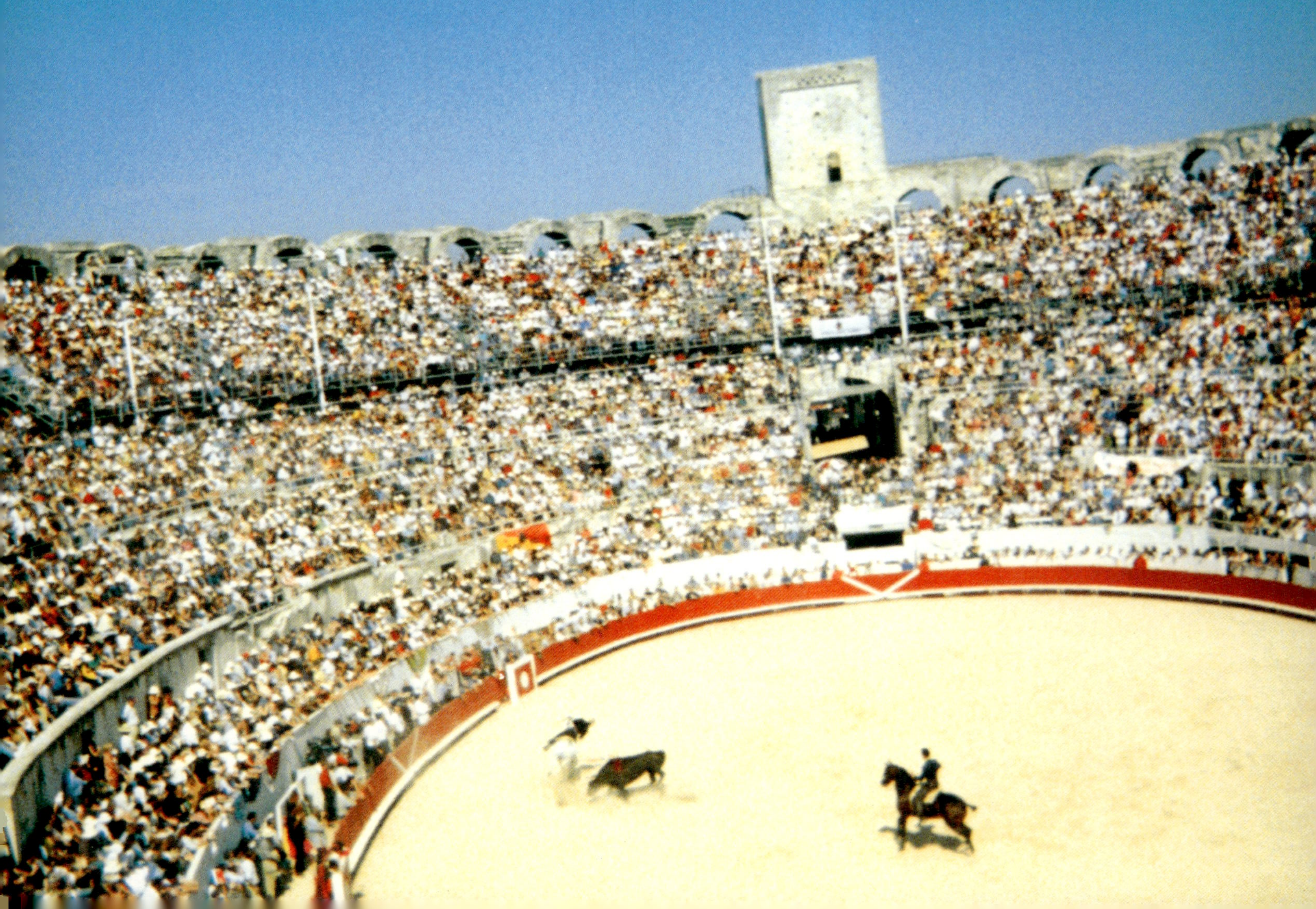

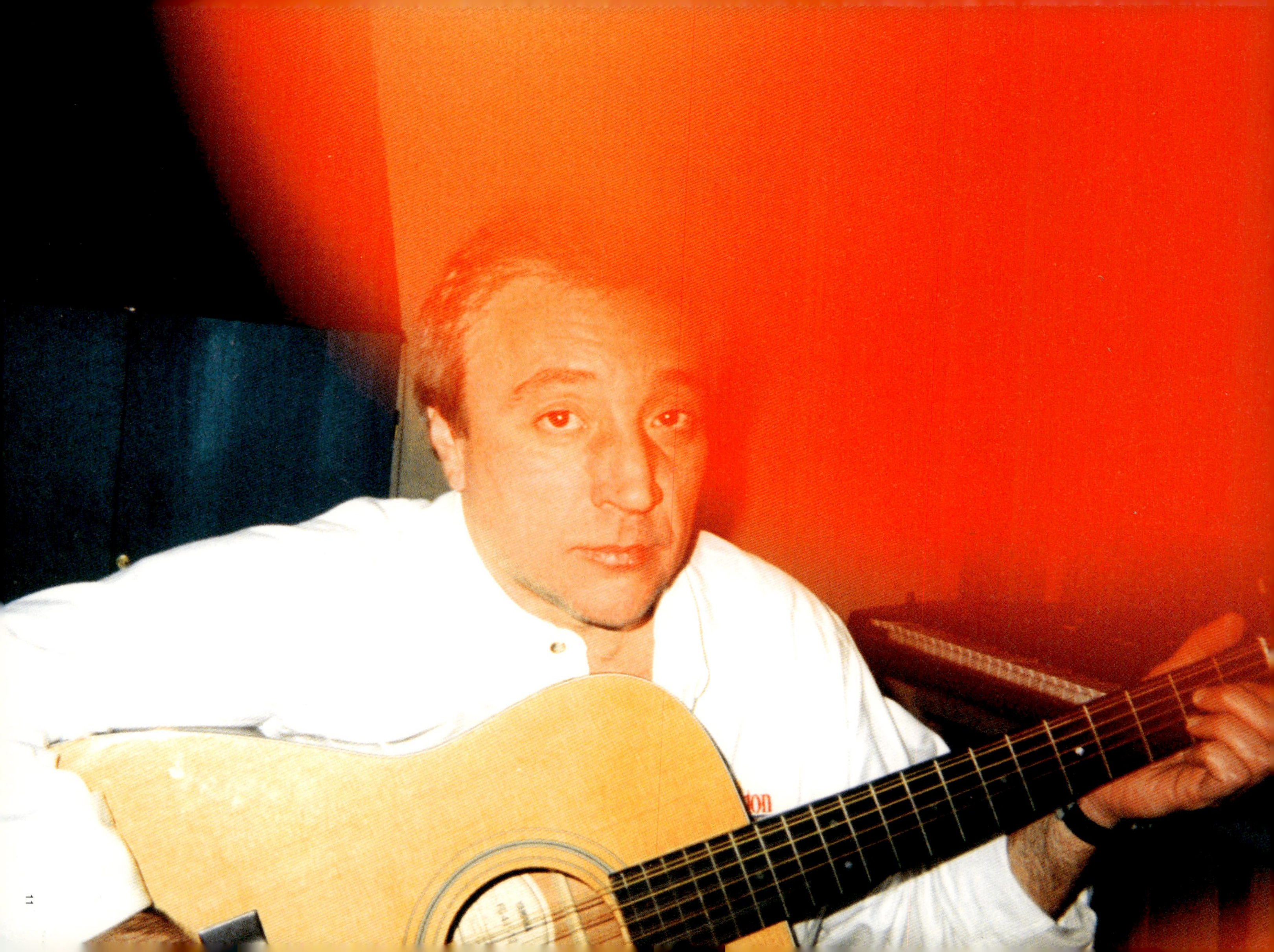

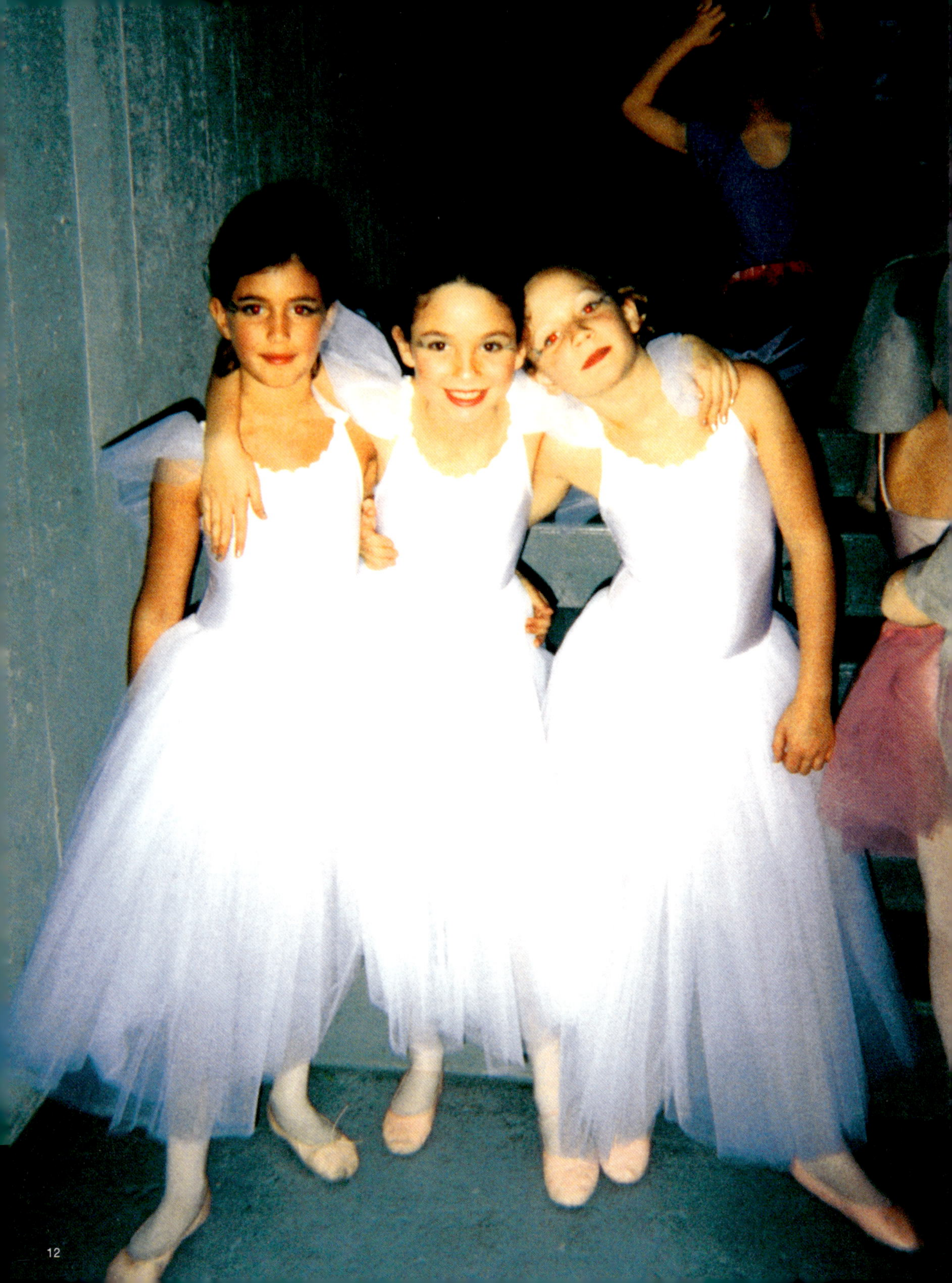

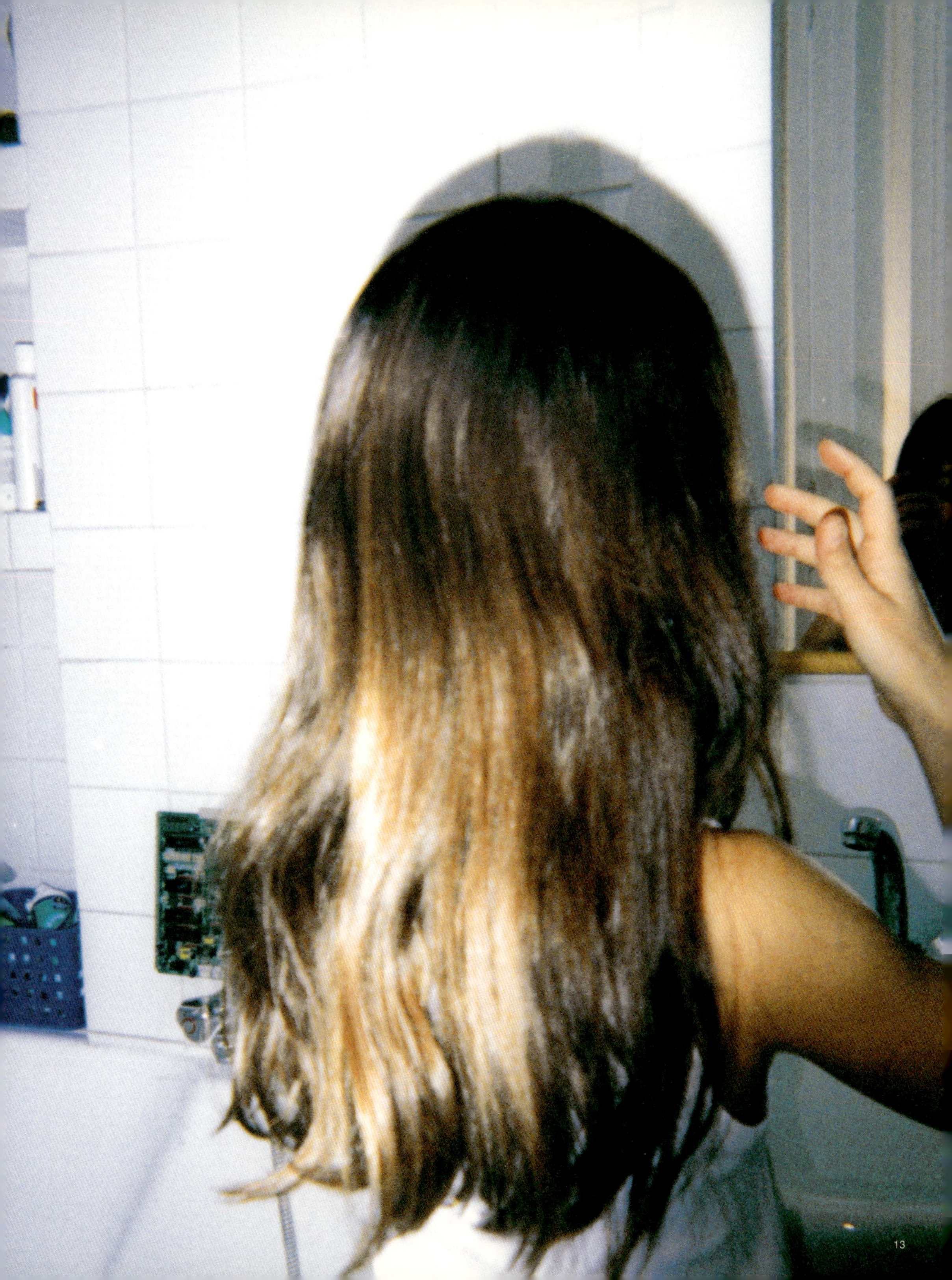

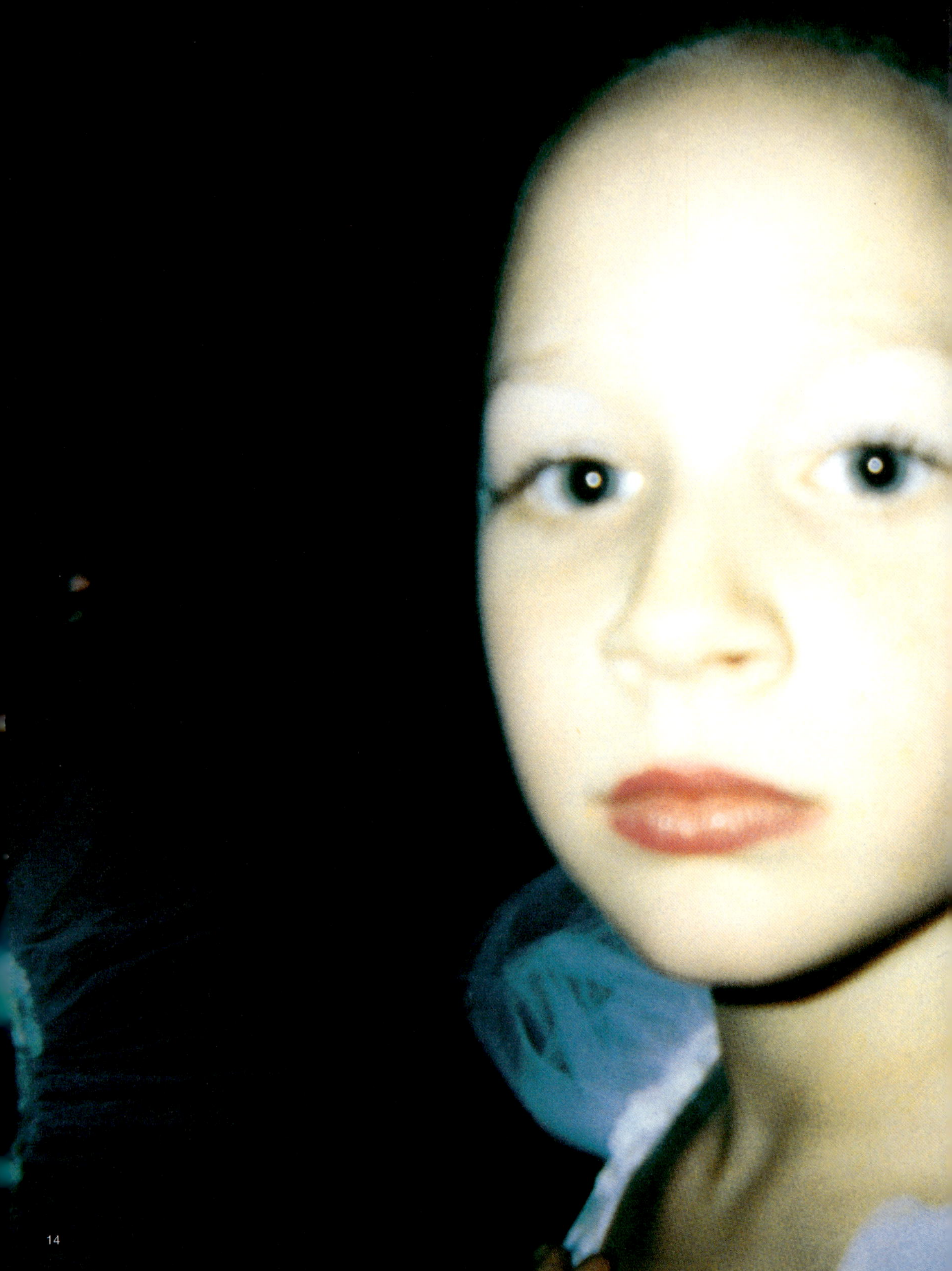

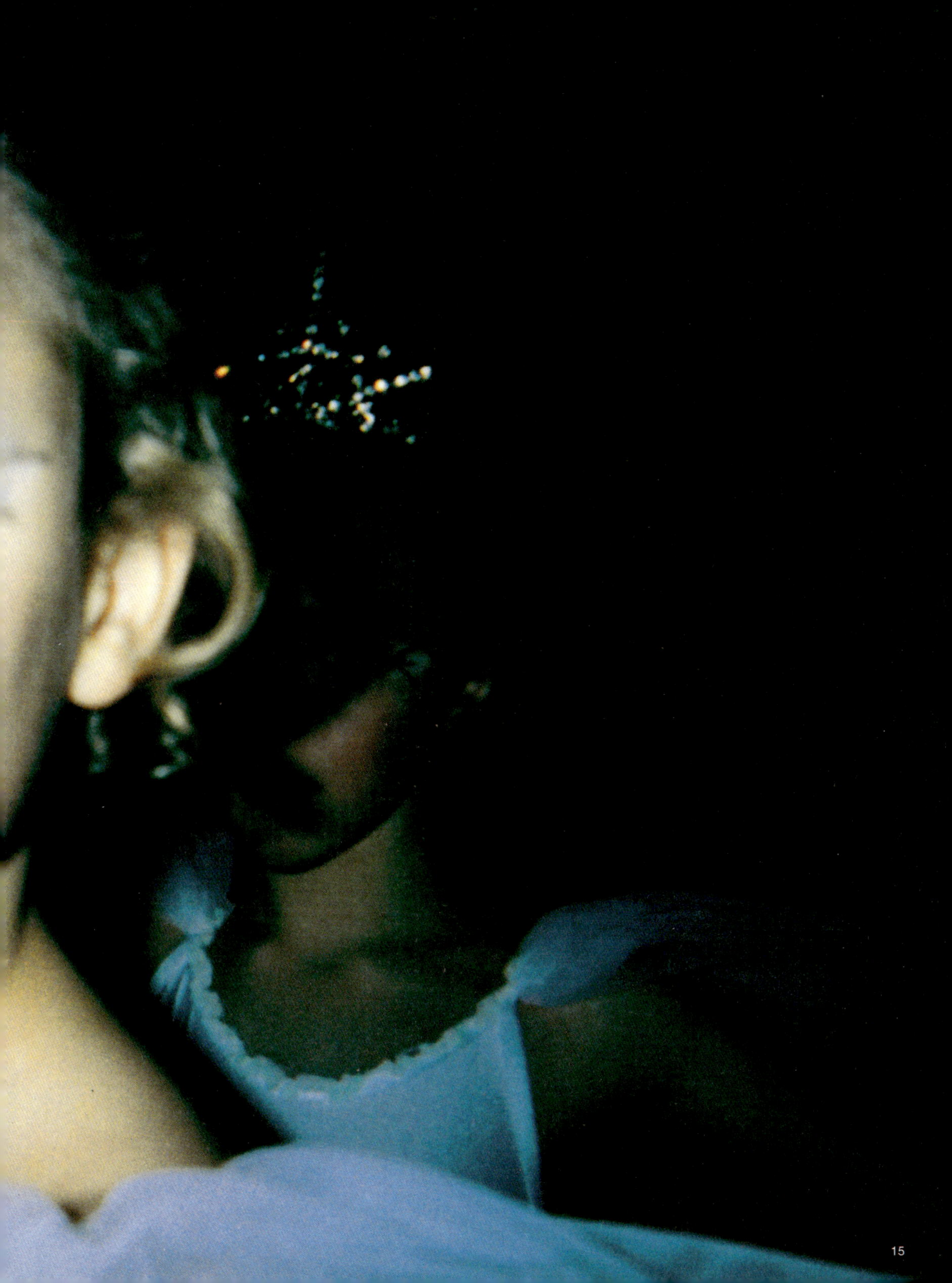

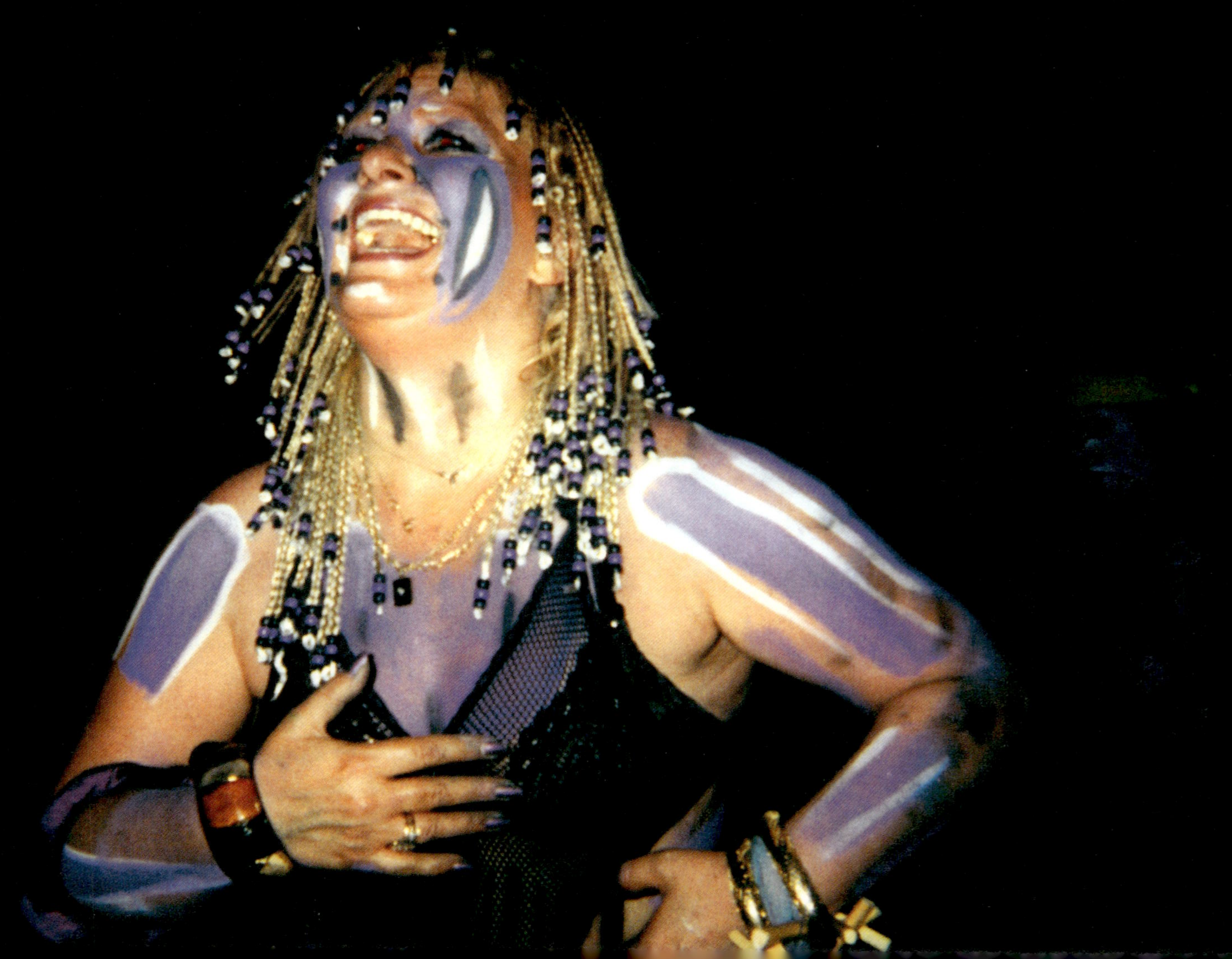

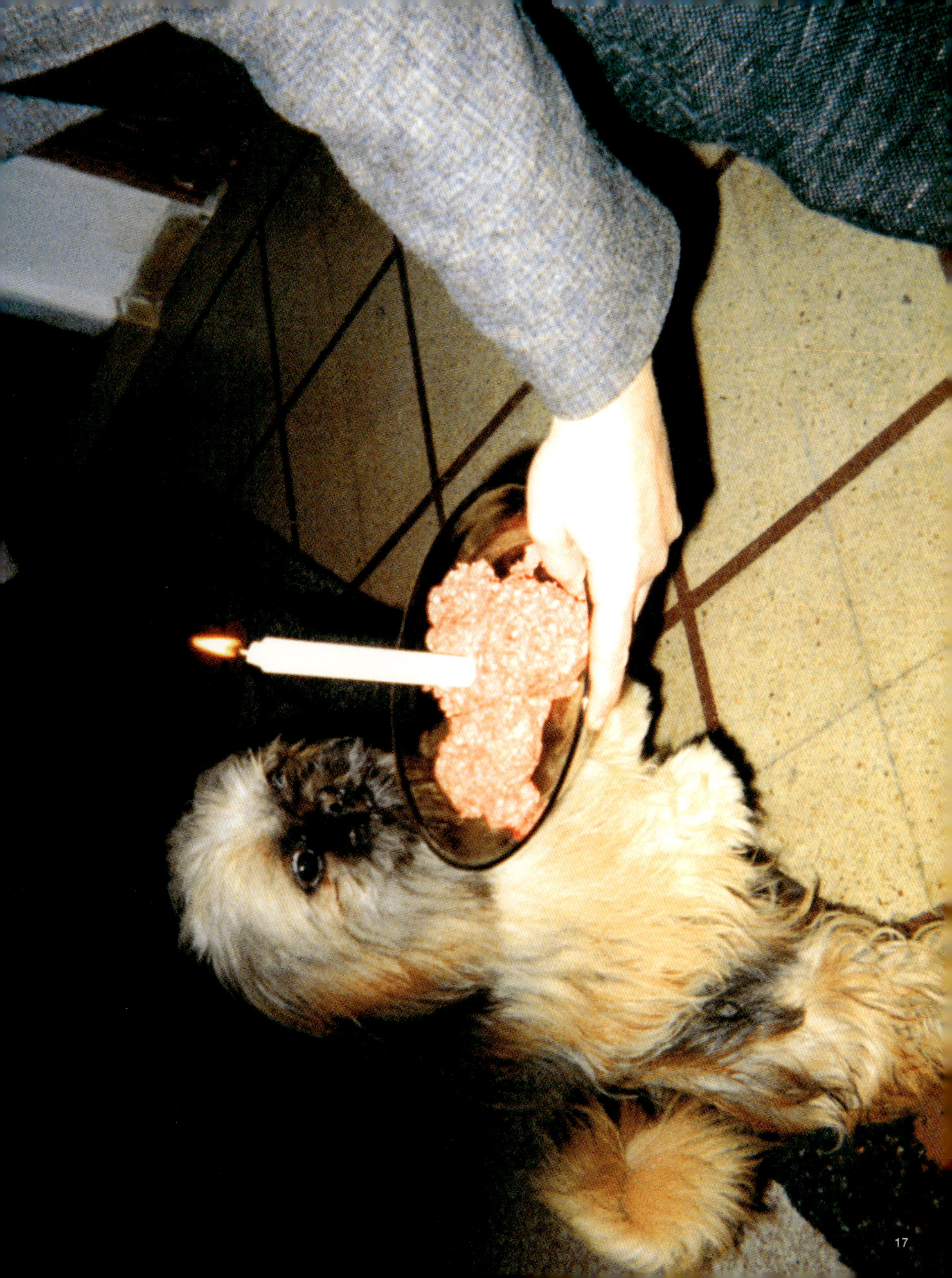

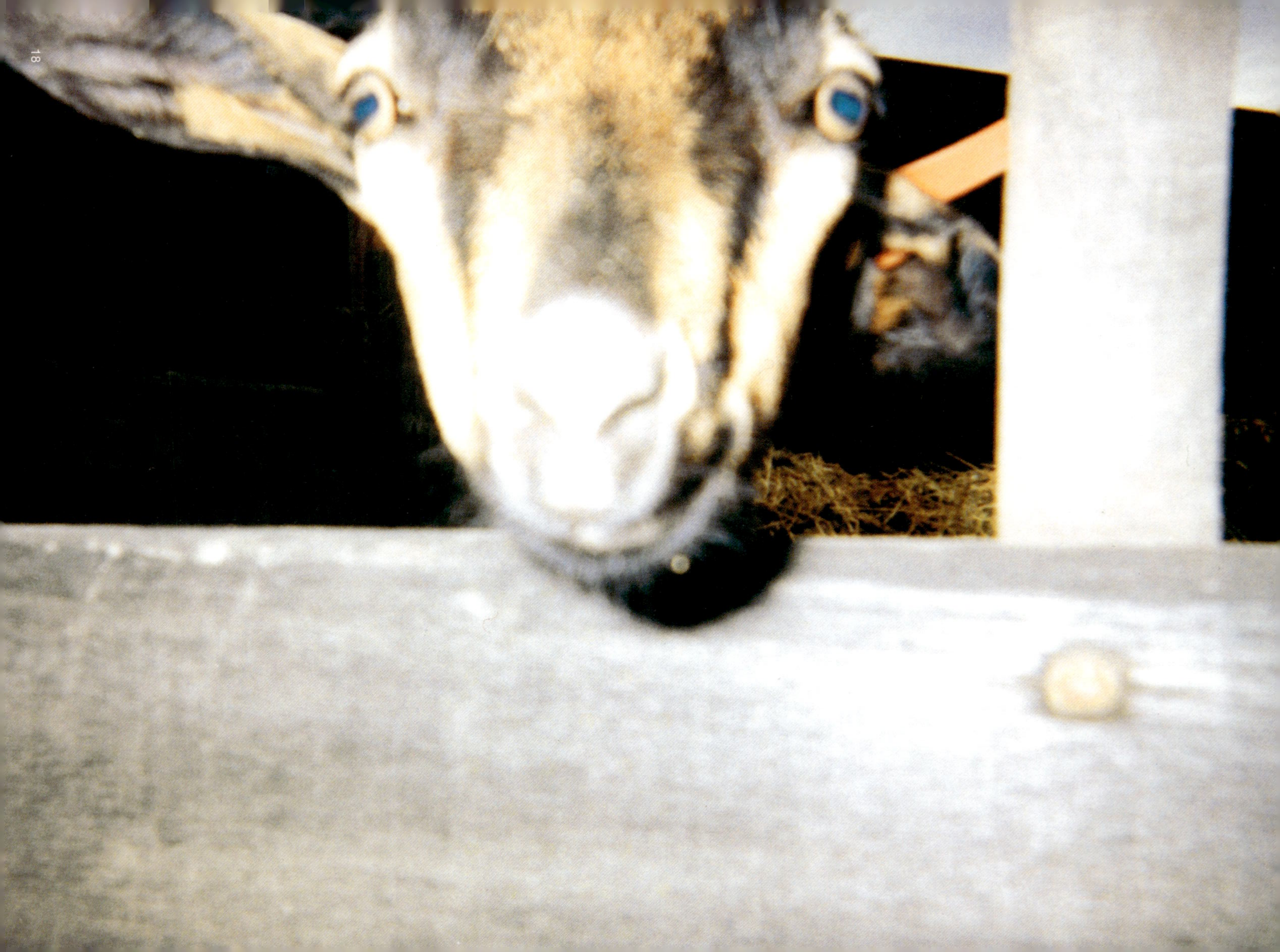

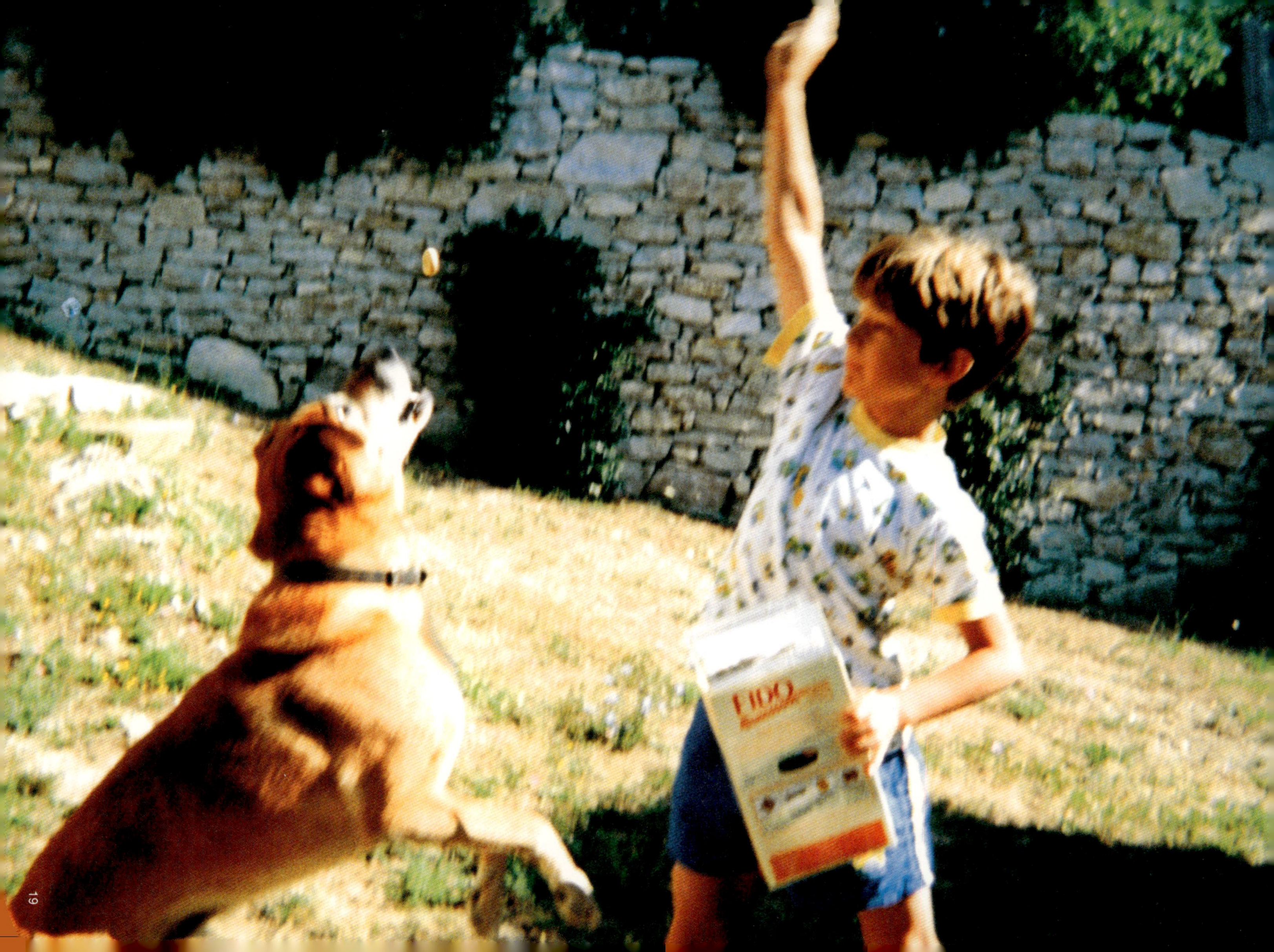

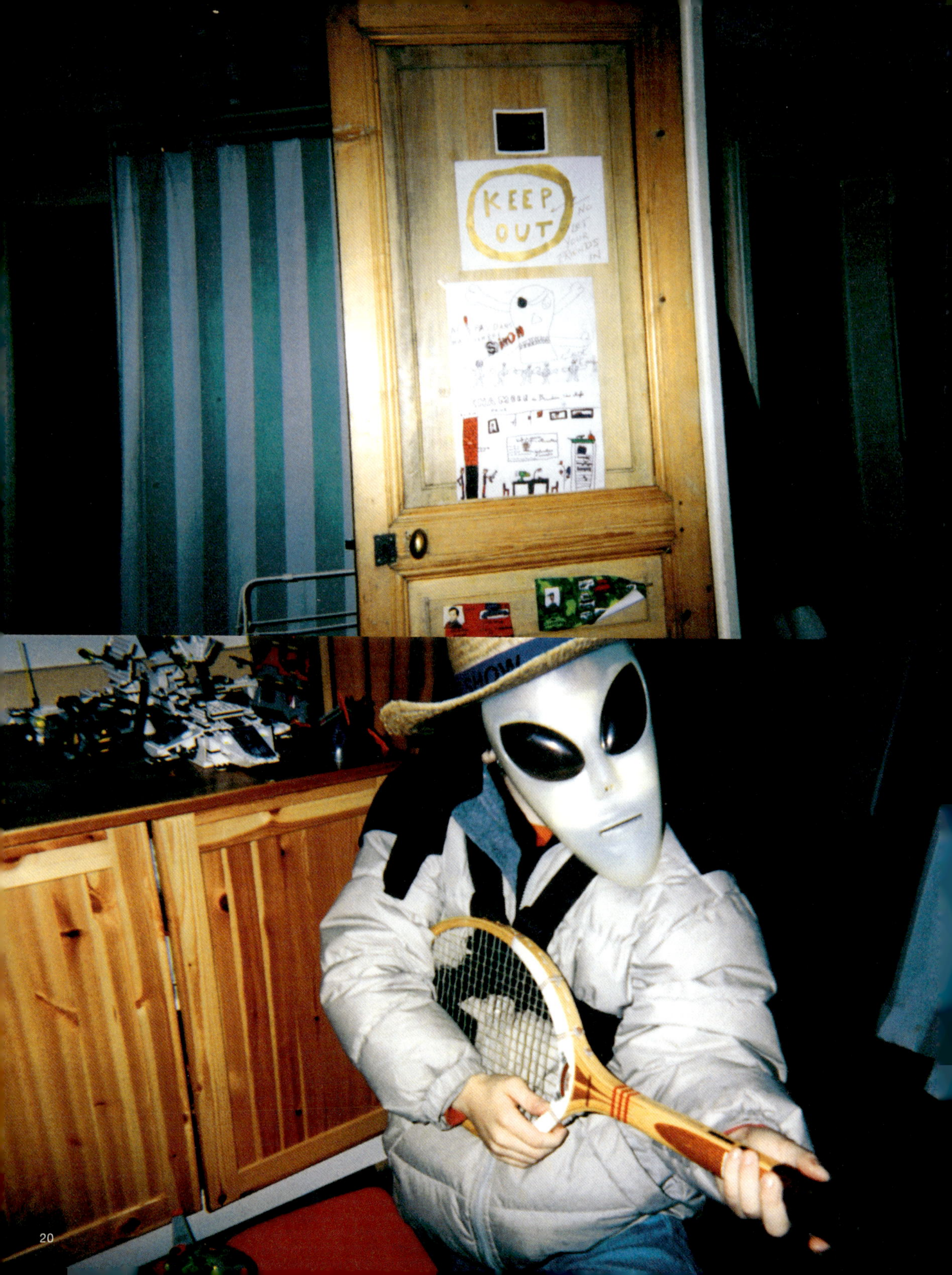
KEEP
OUT

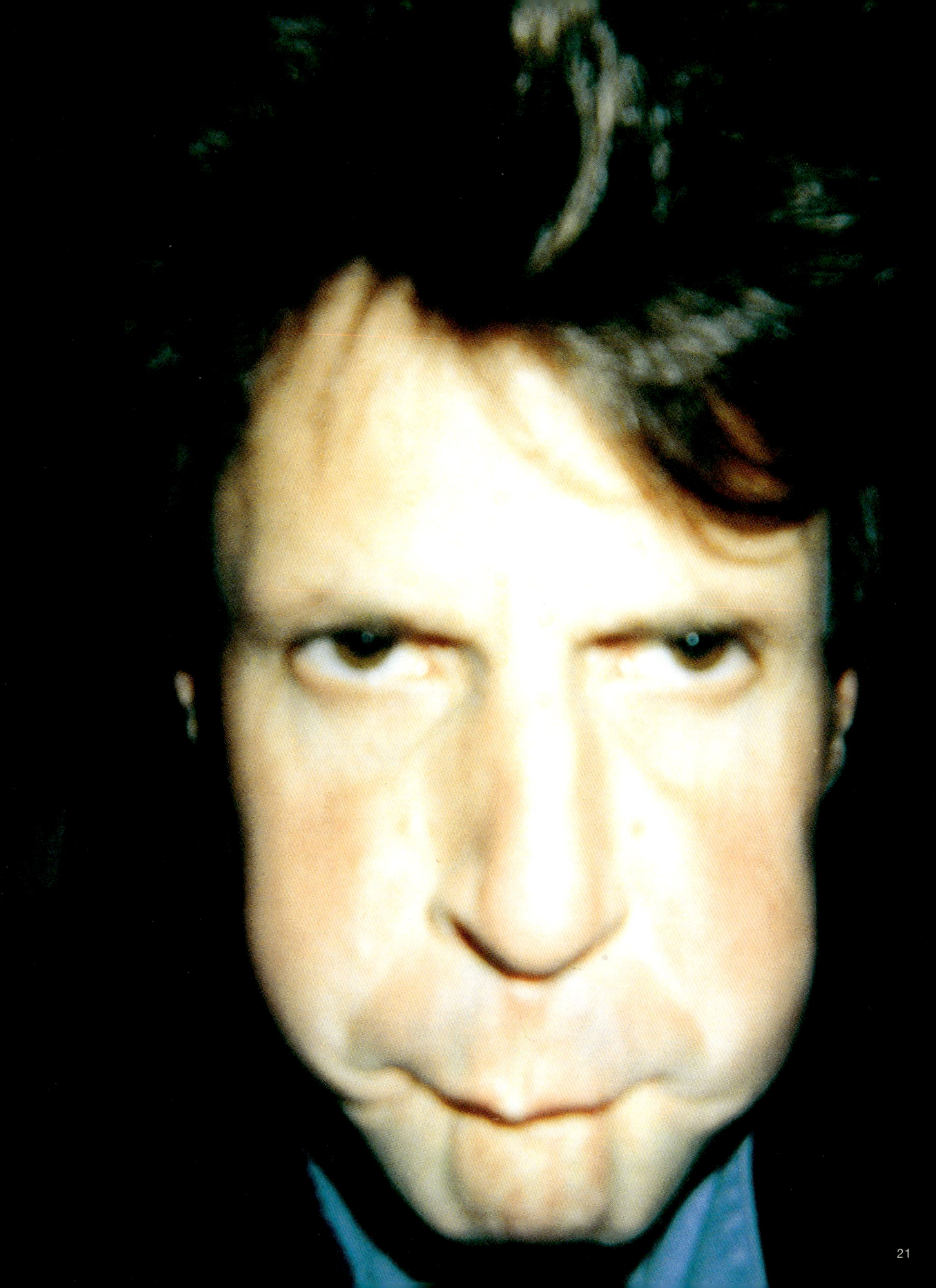

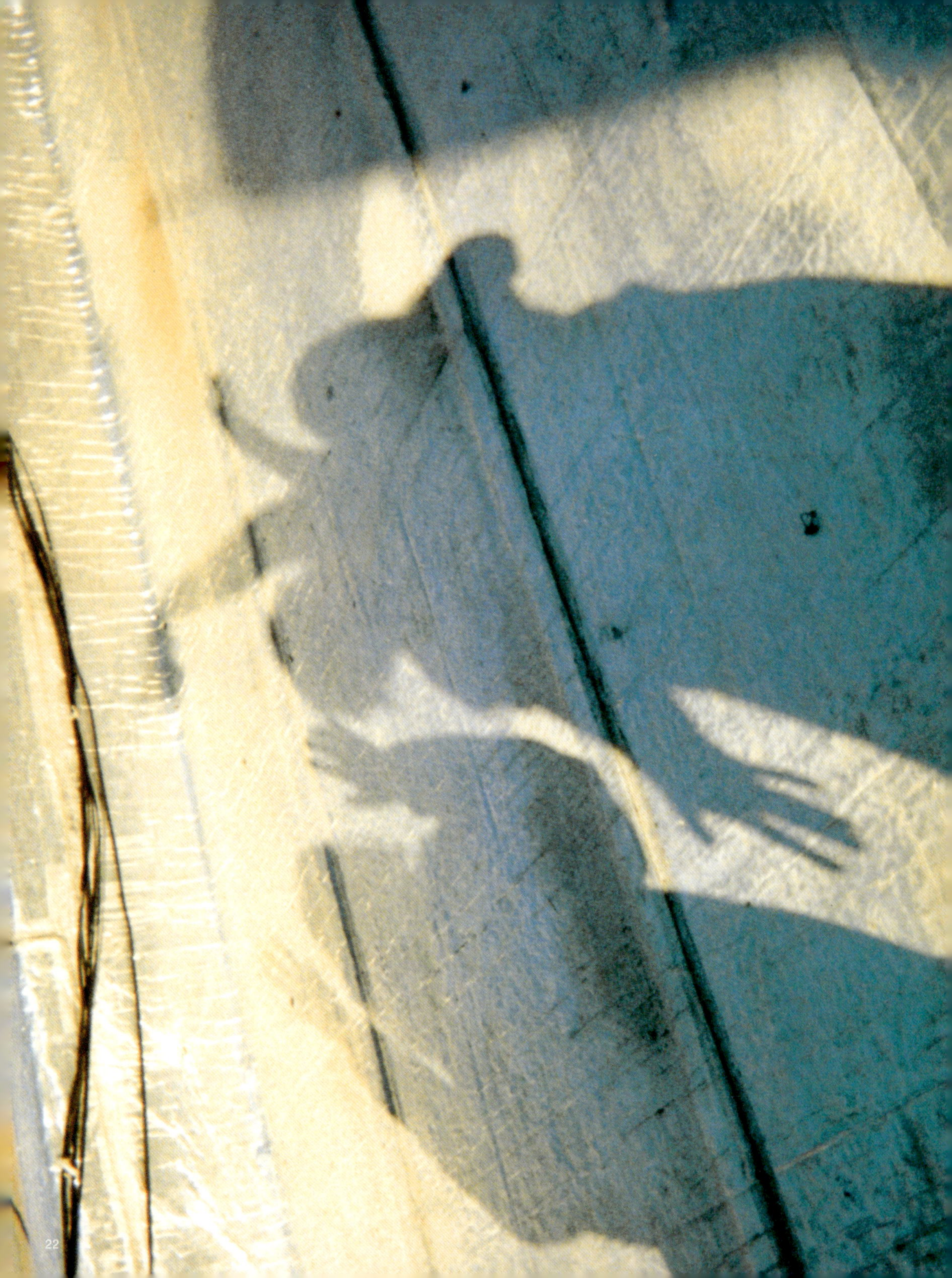

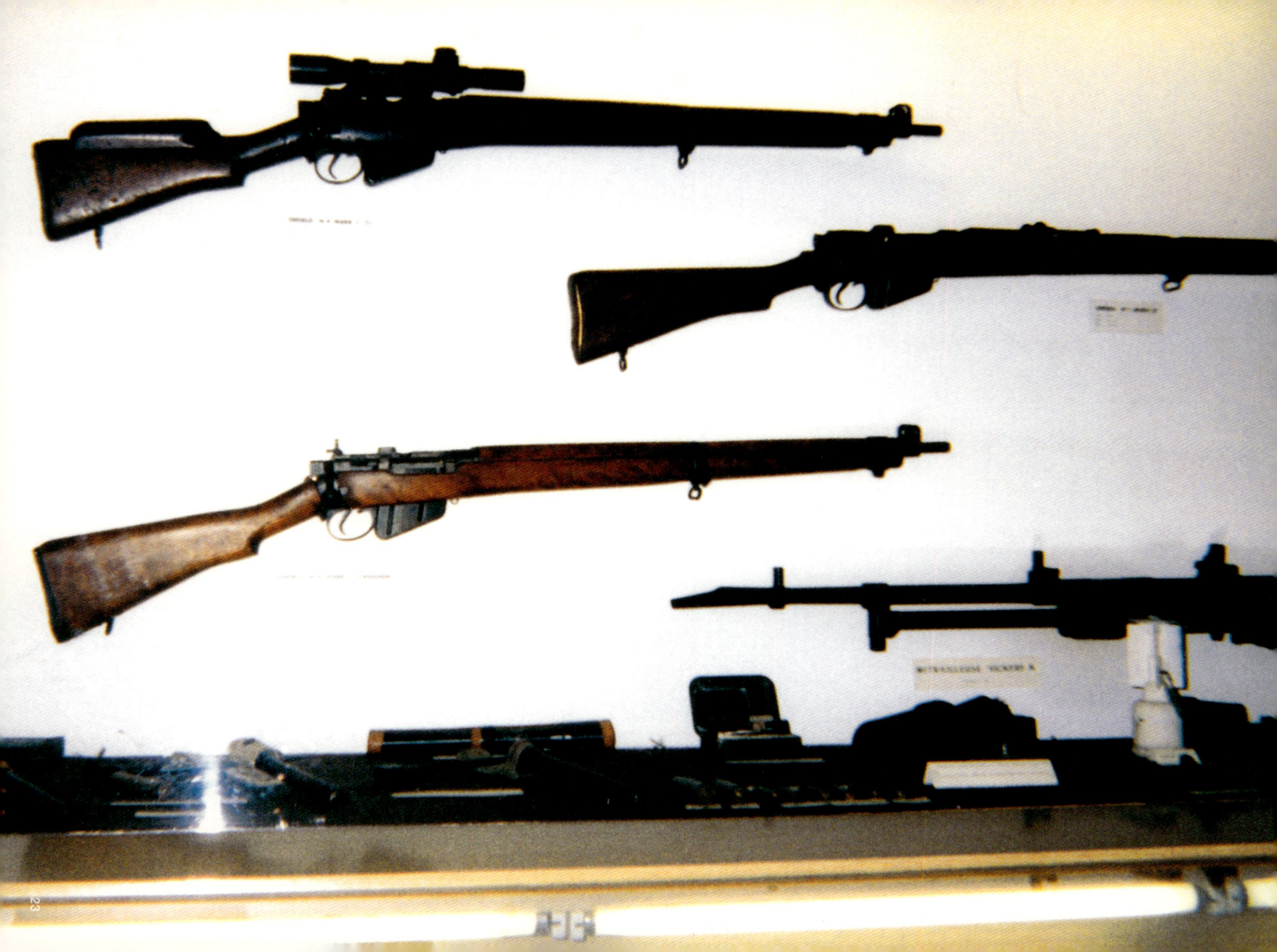

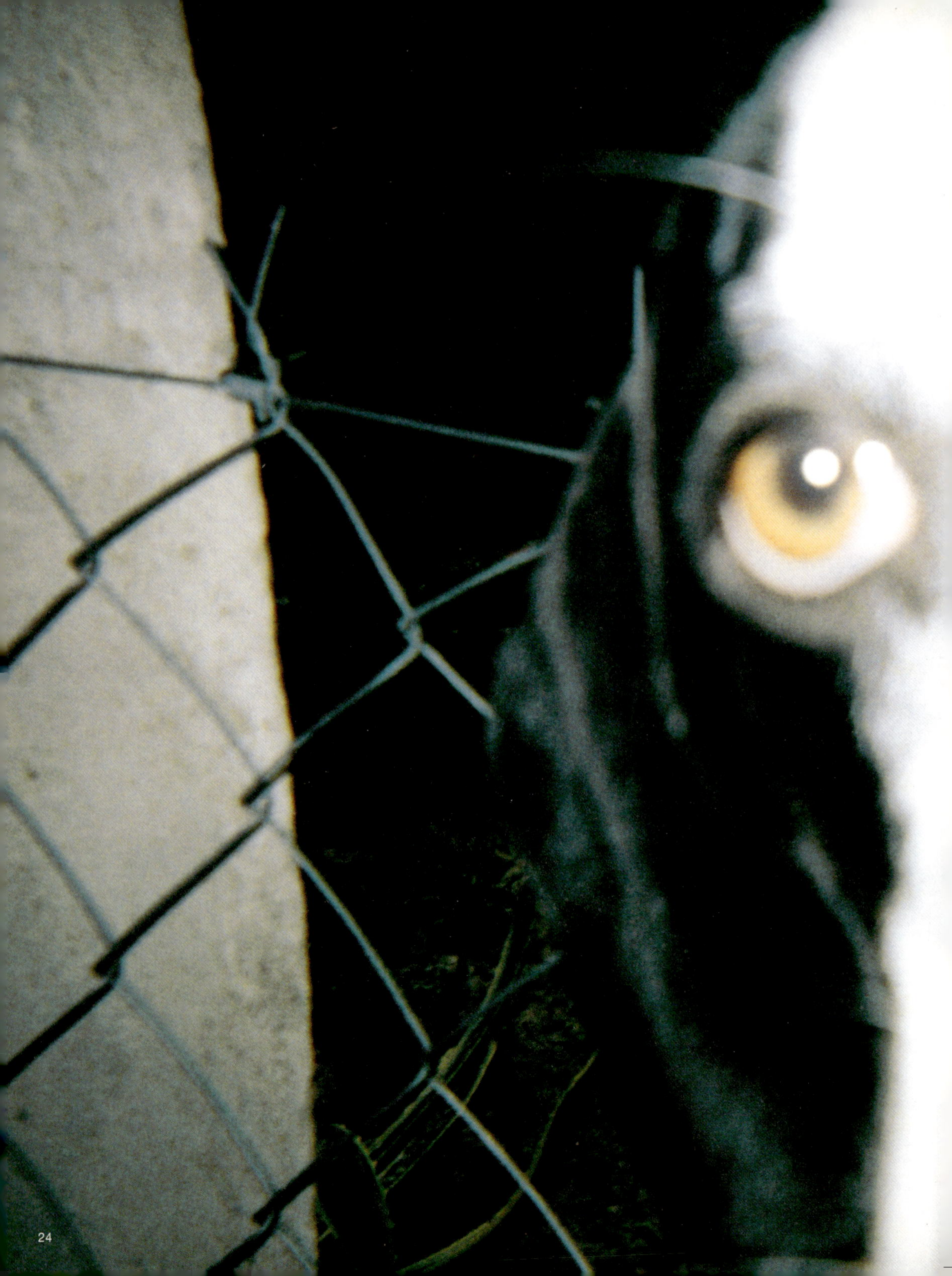

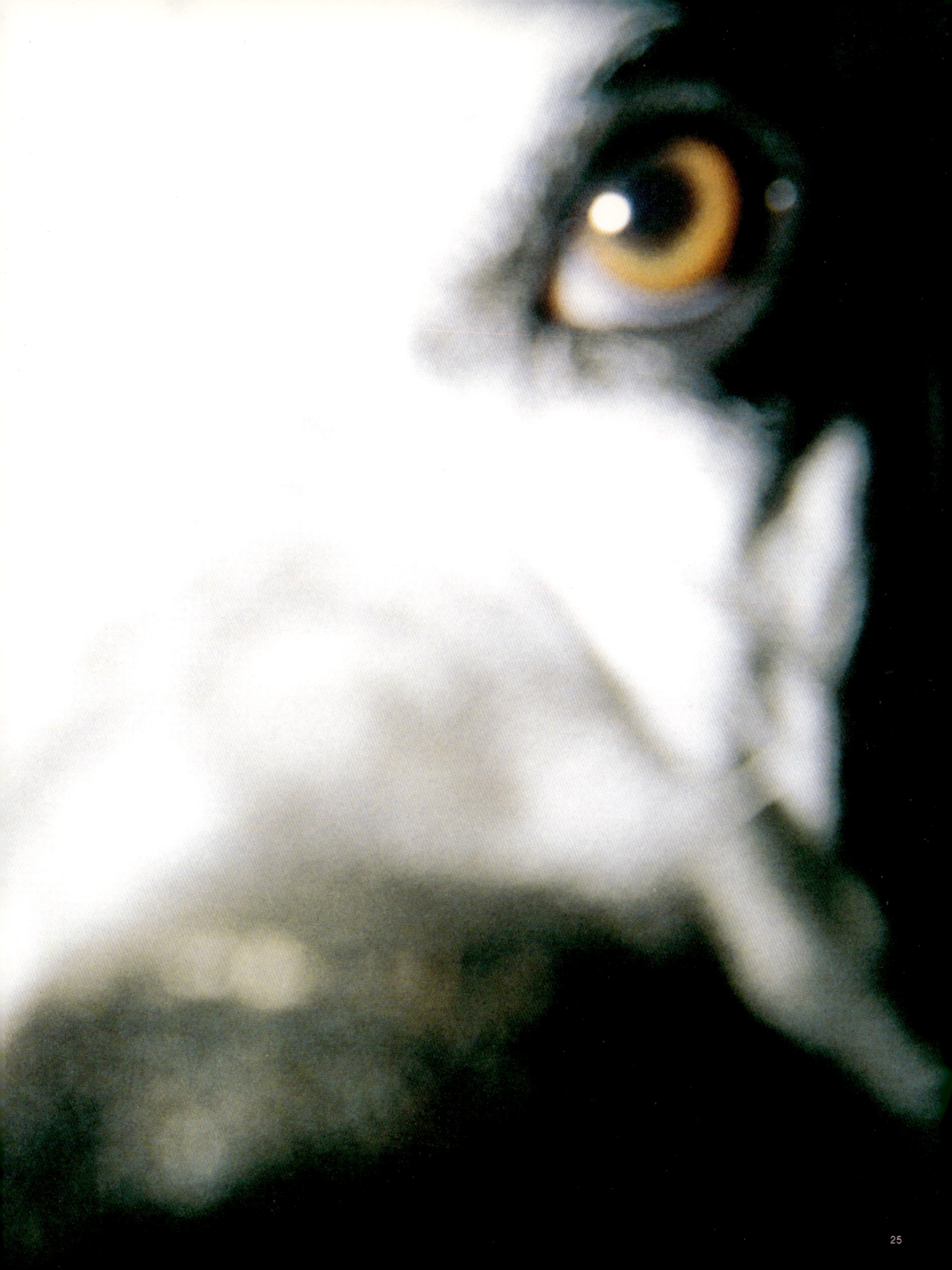

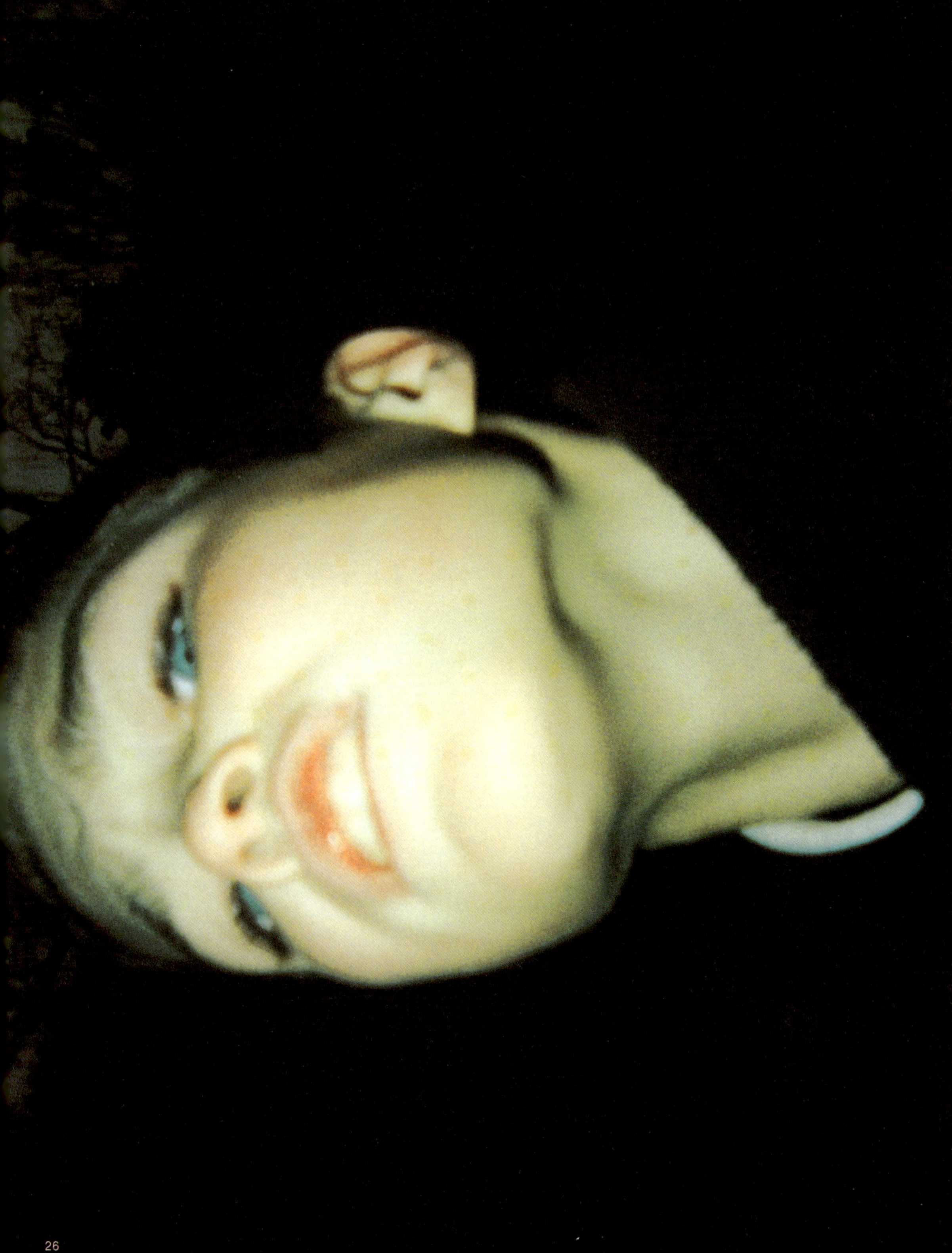

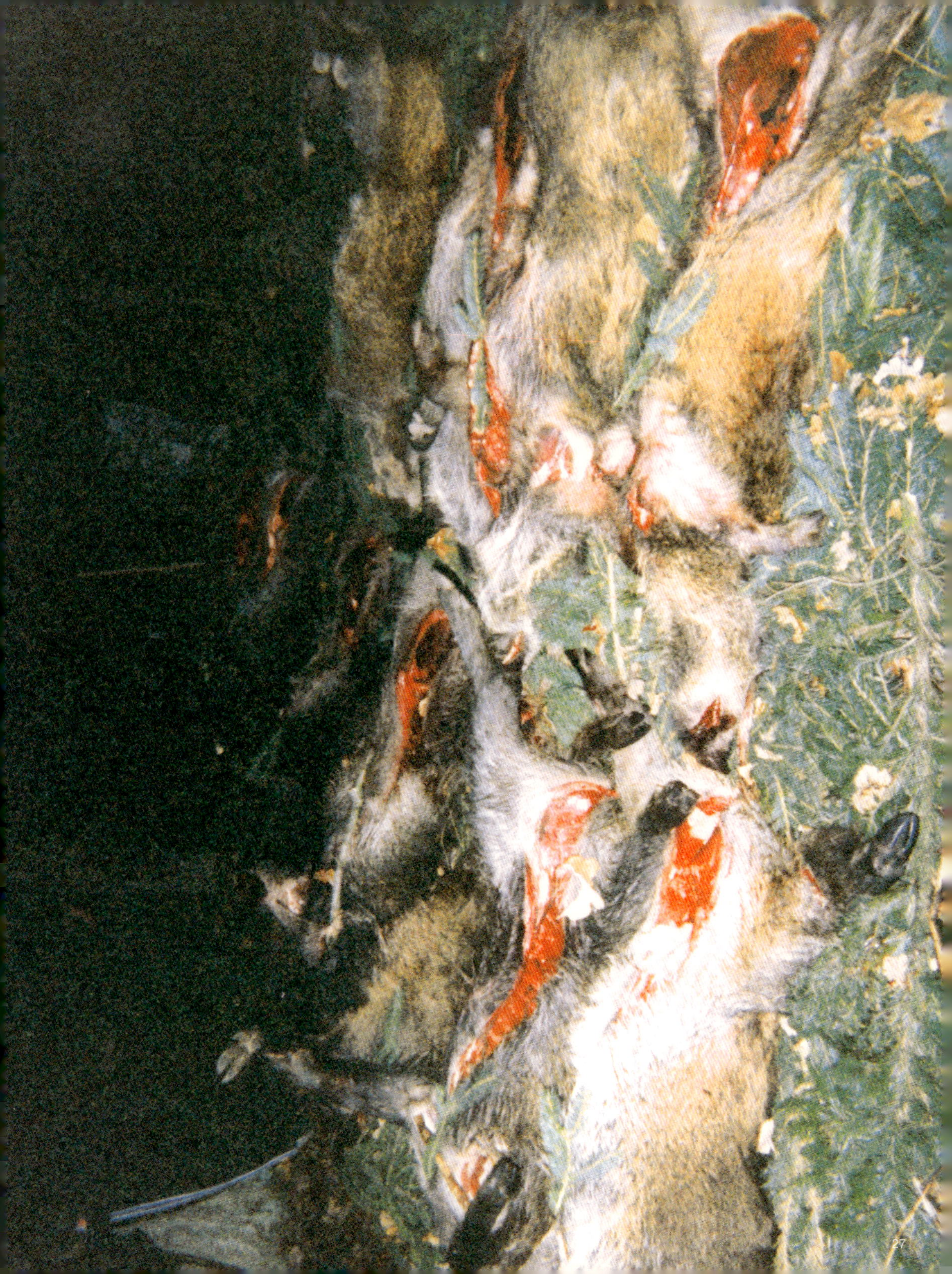

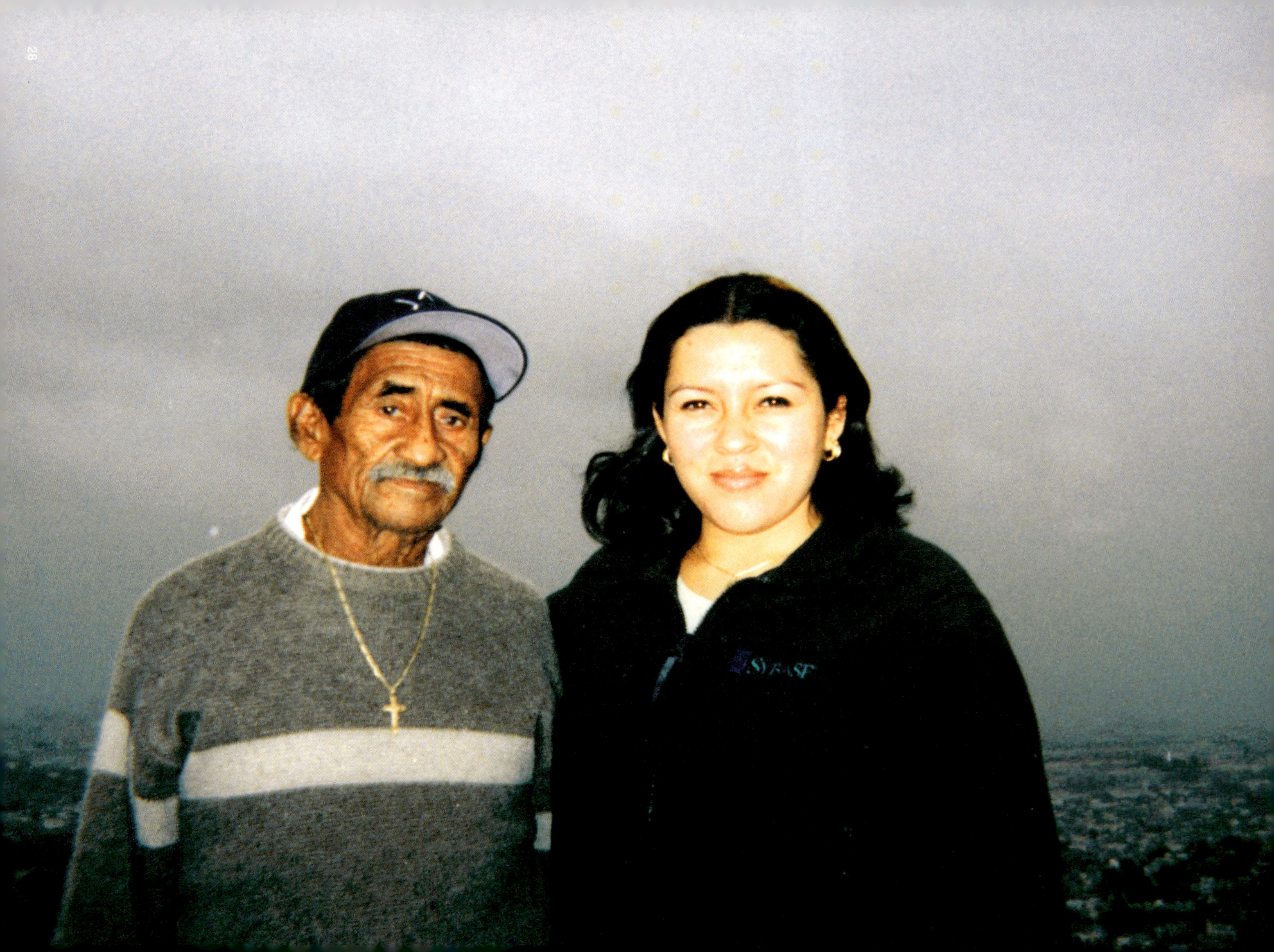

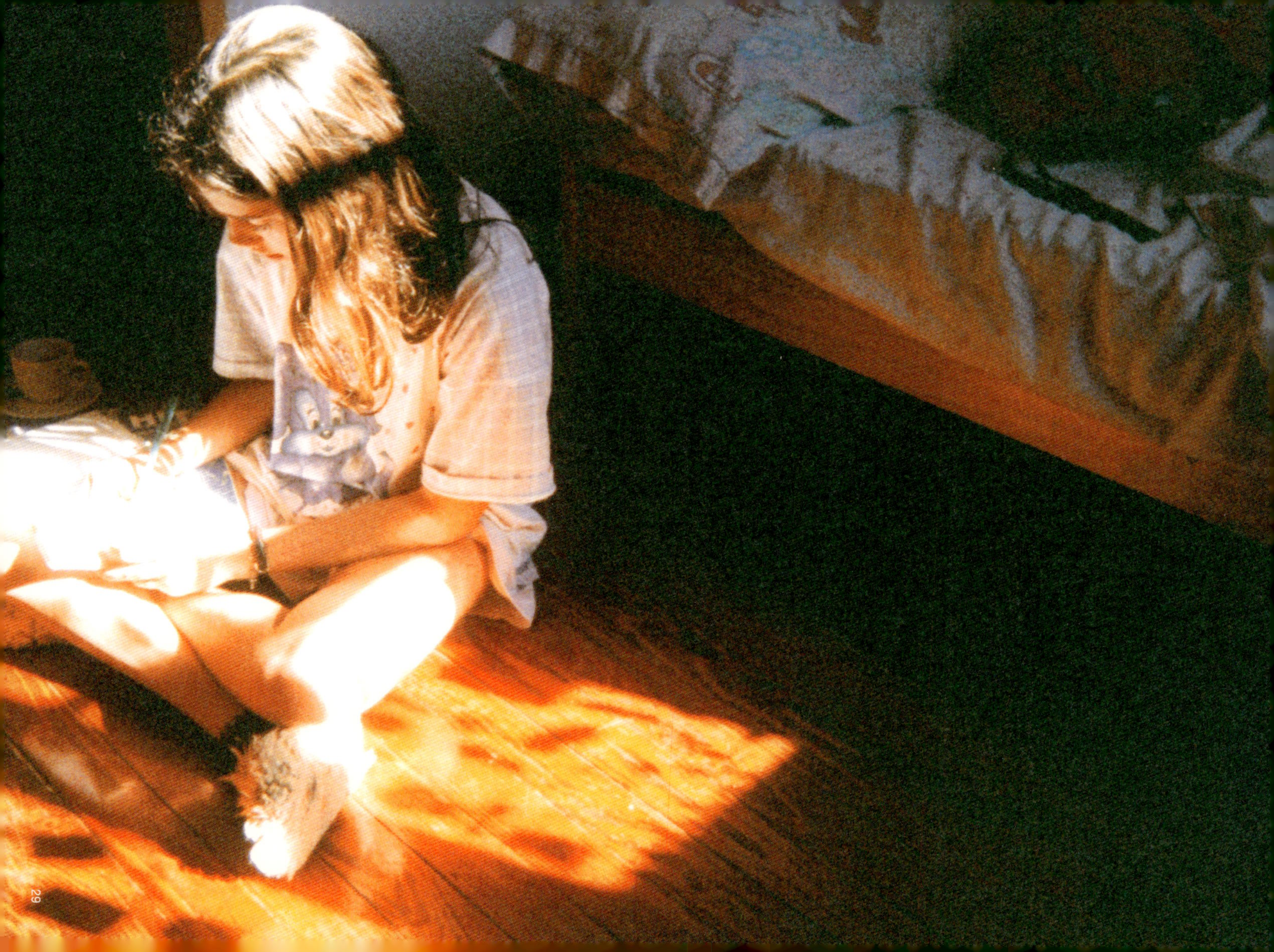

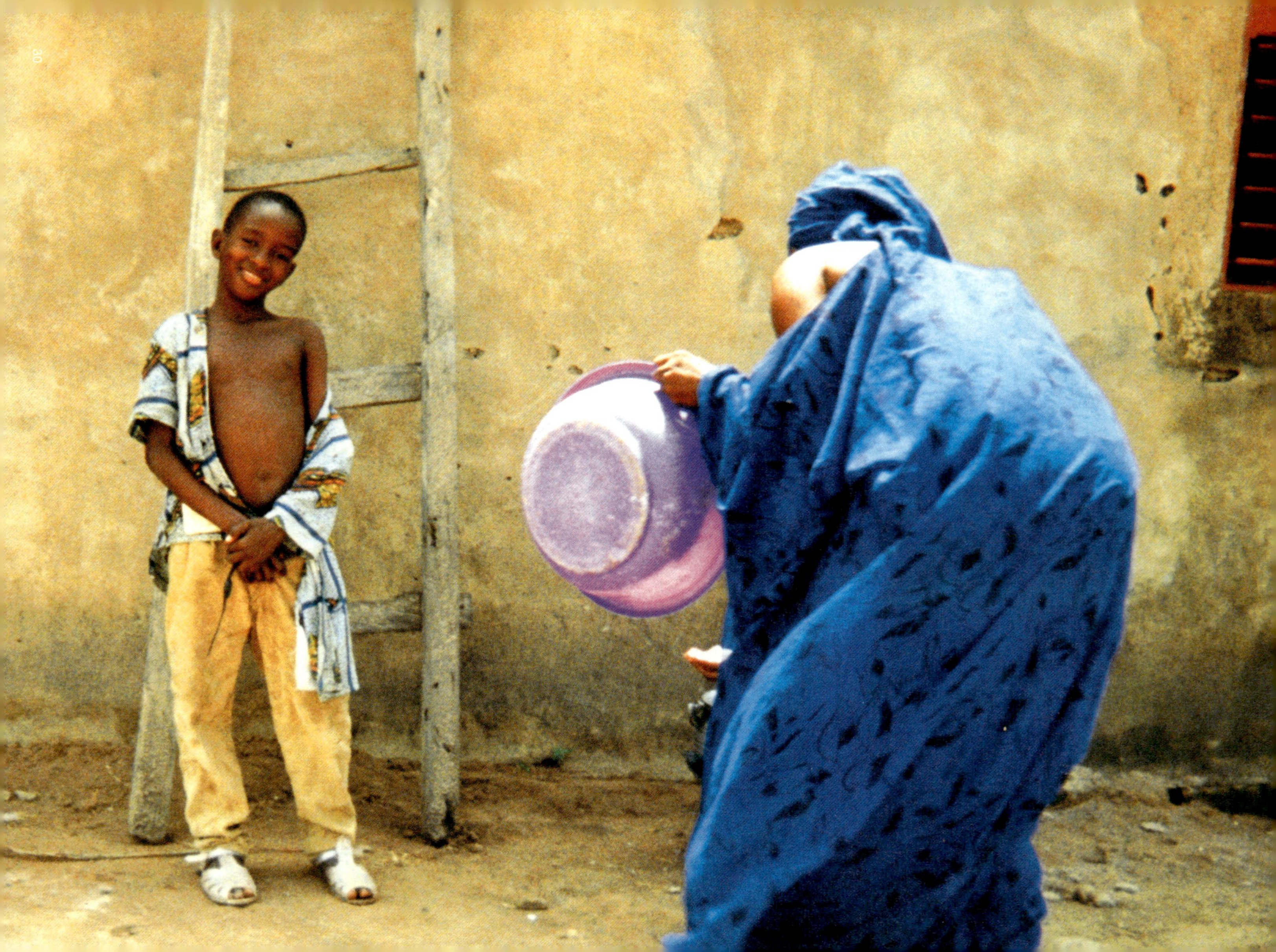

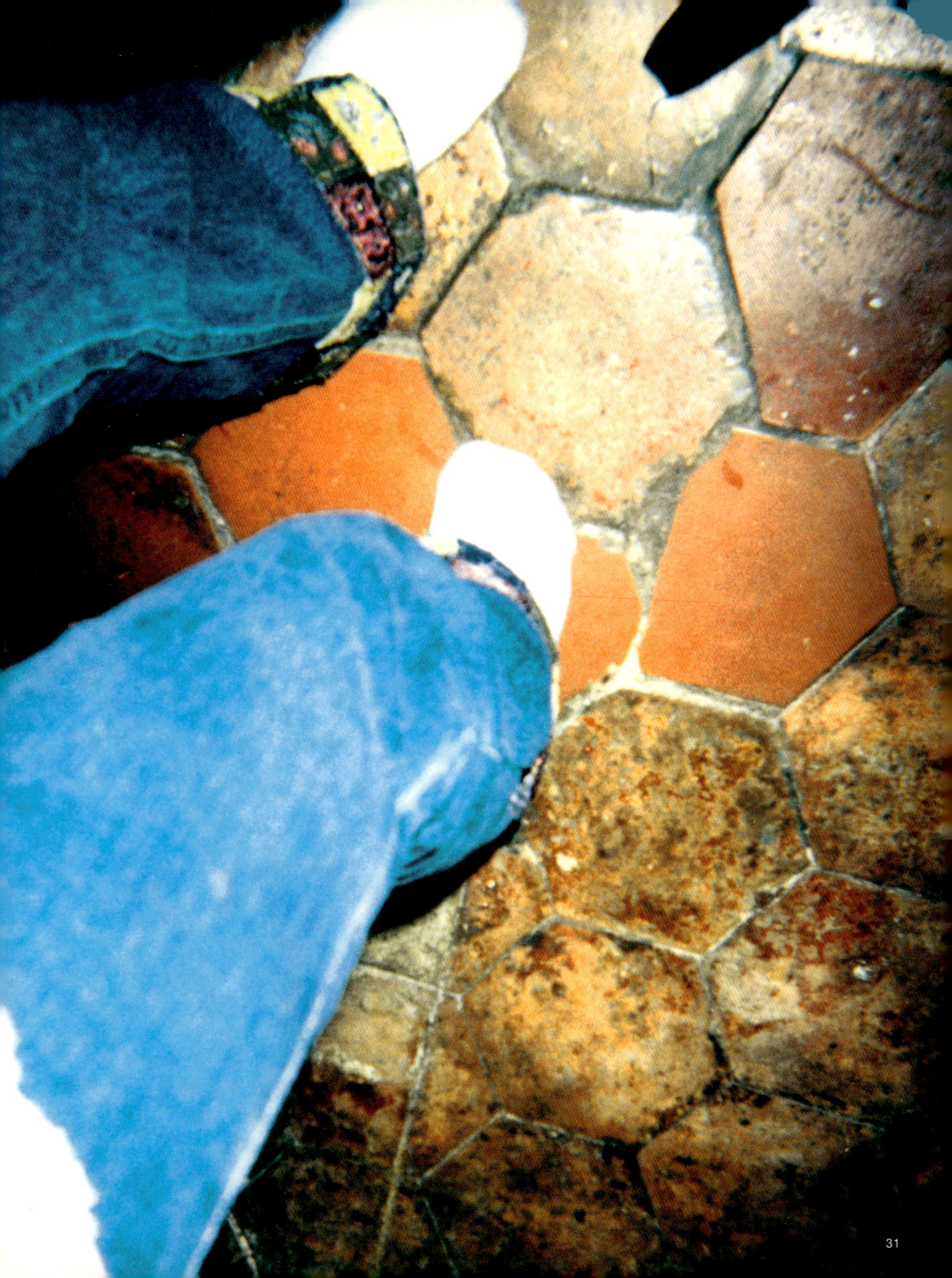

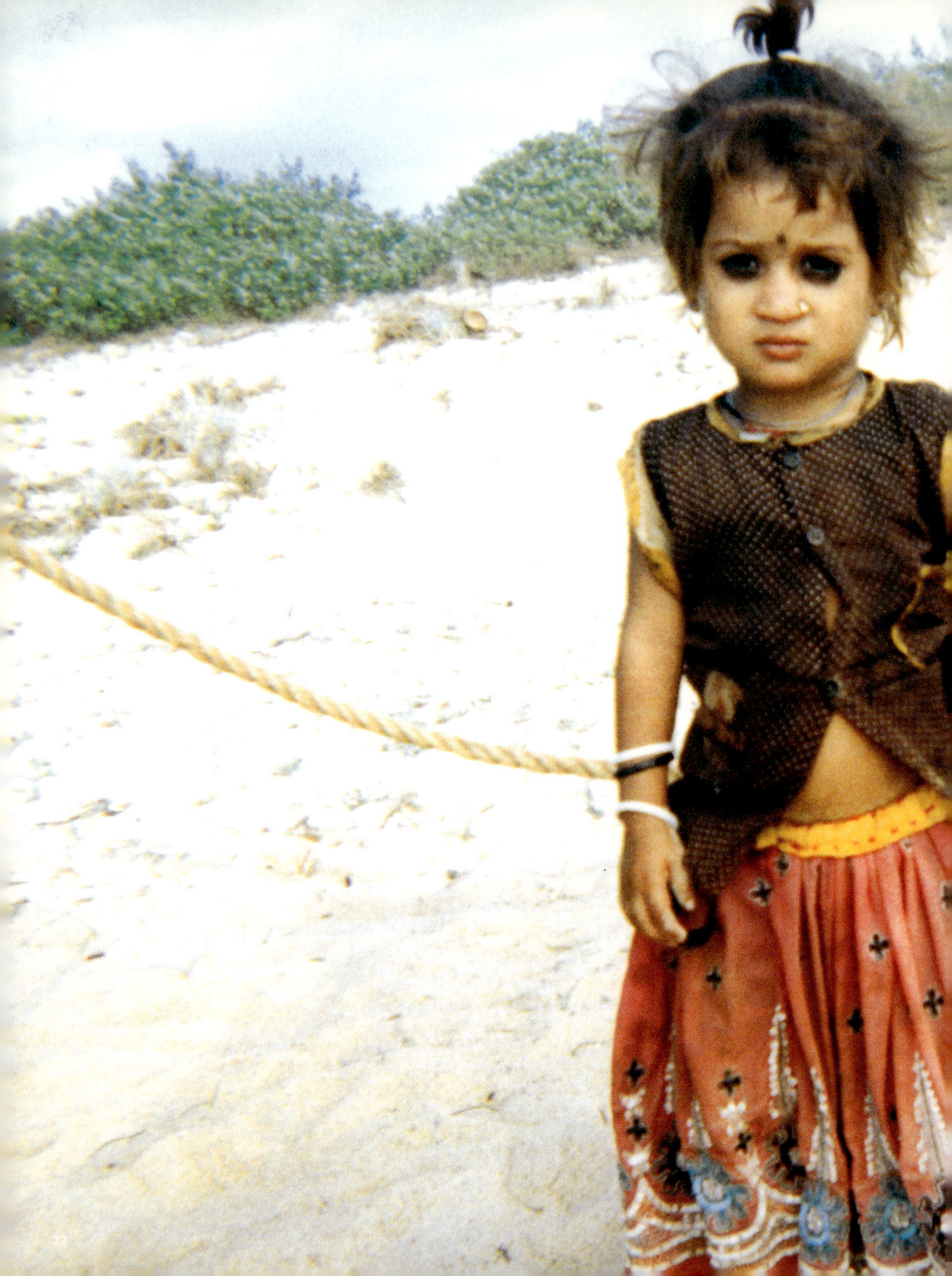

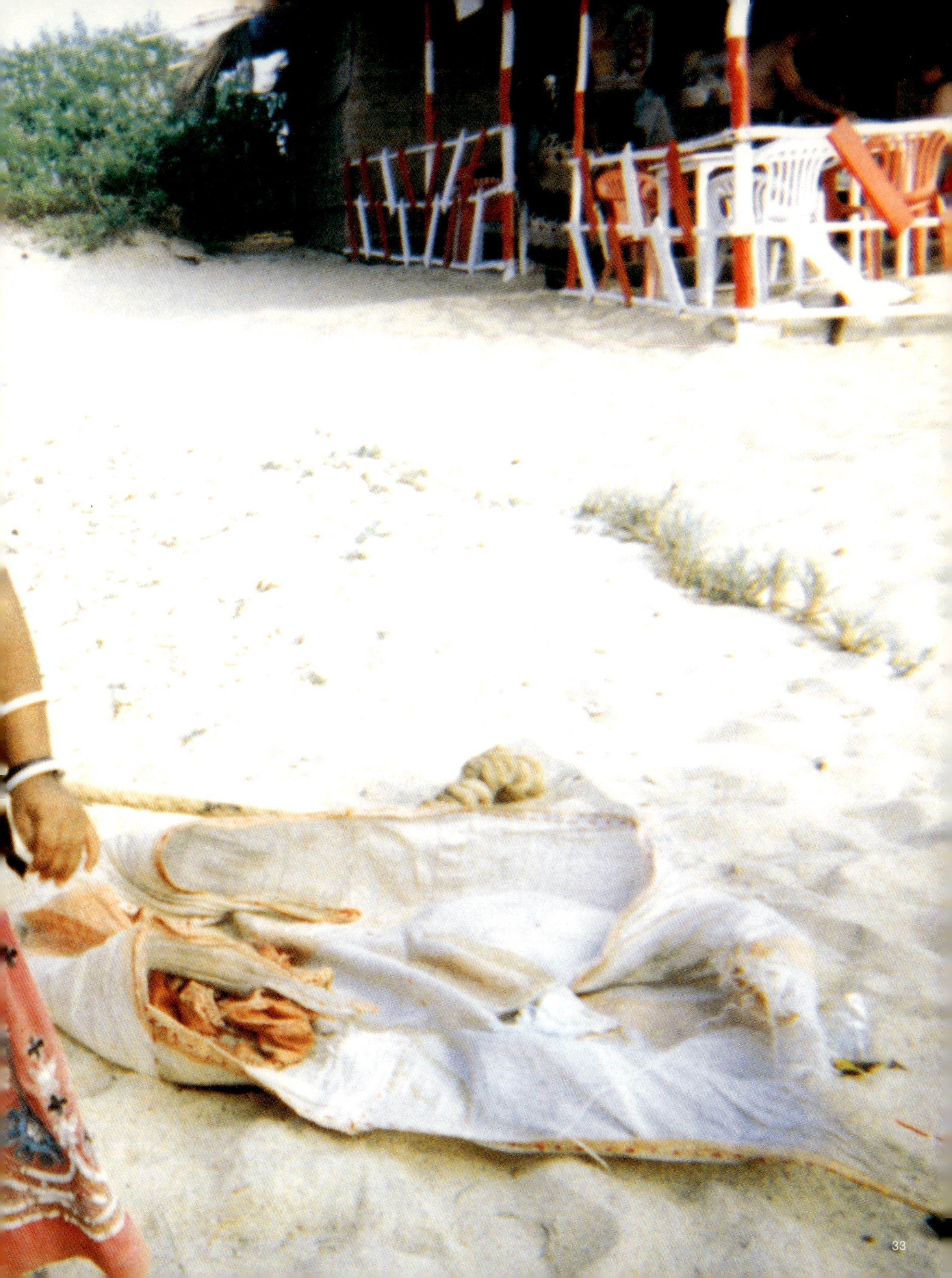

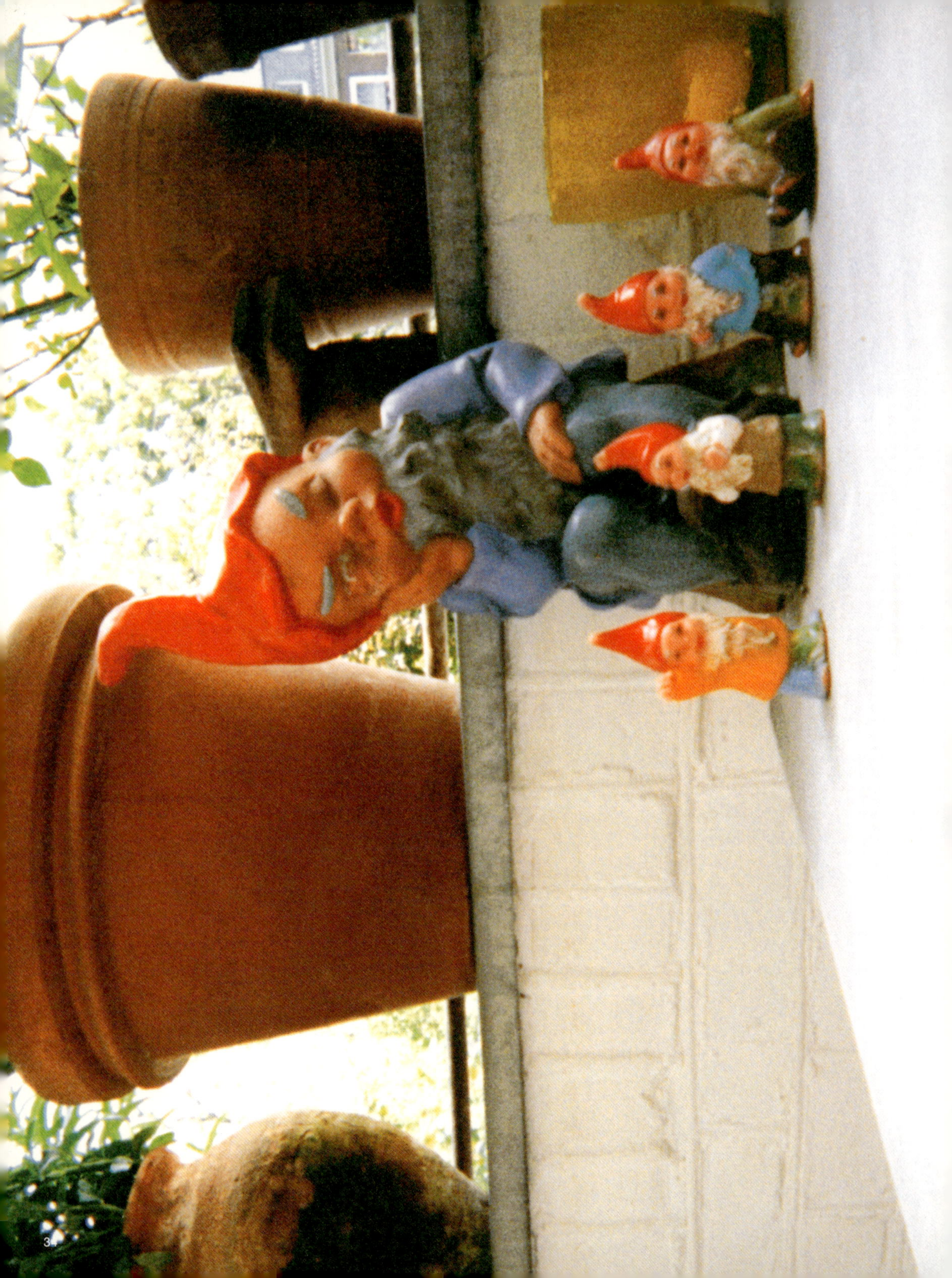

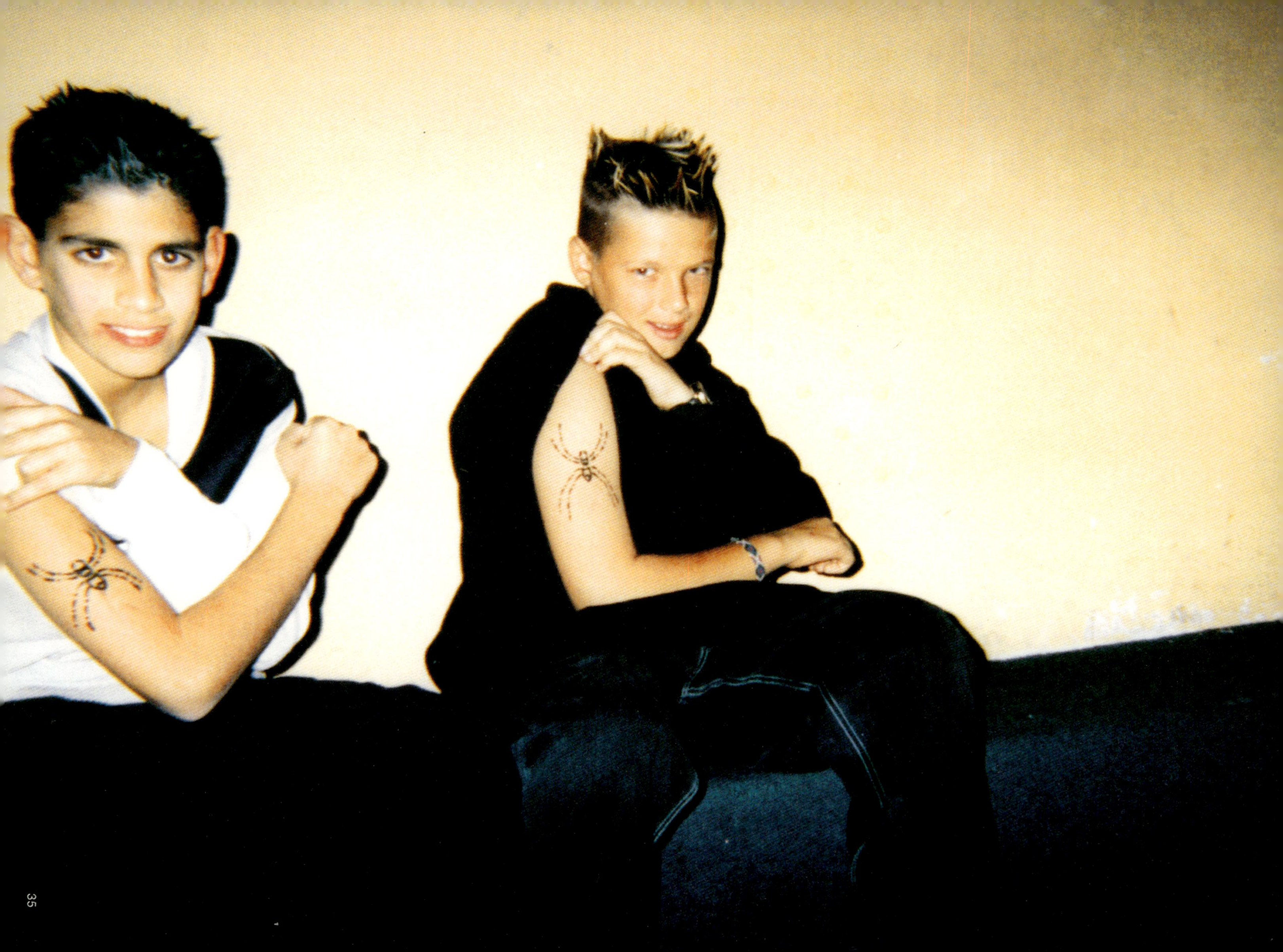

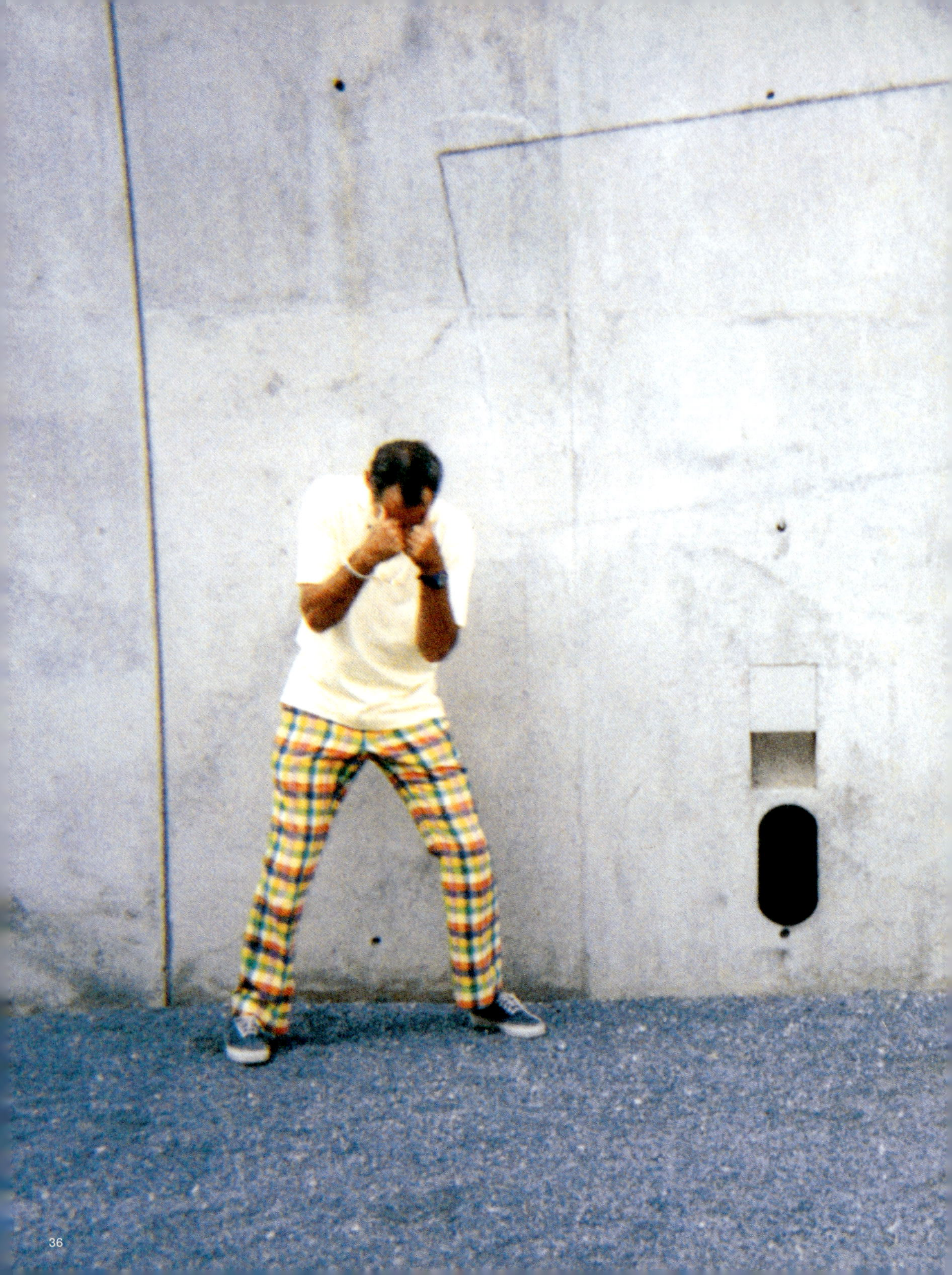

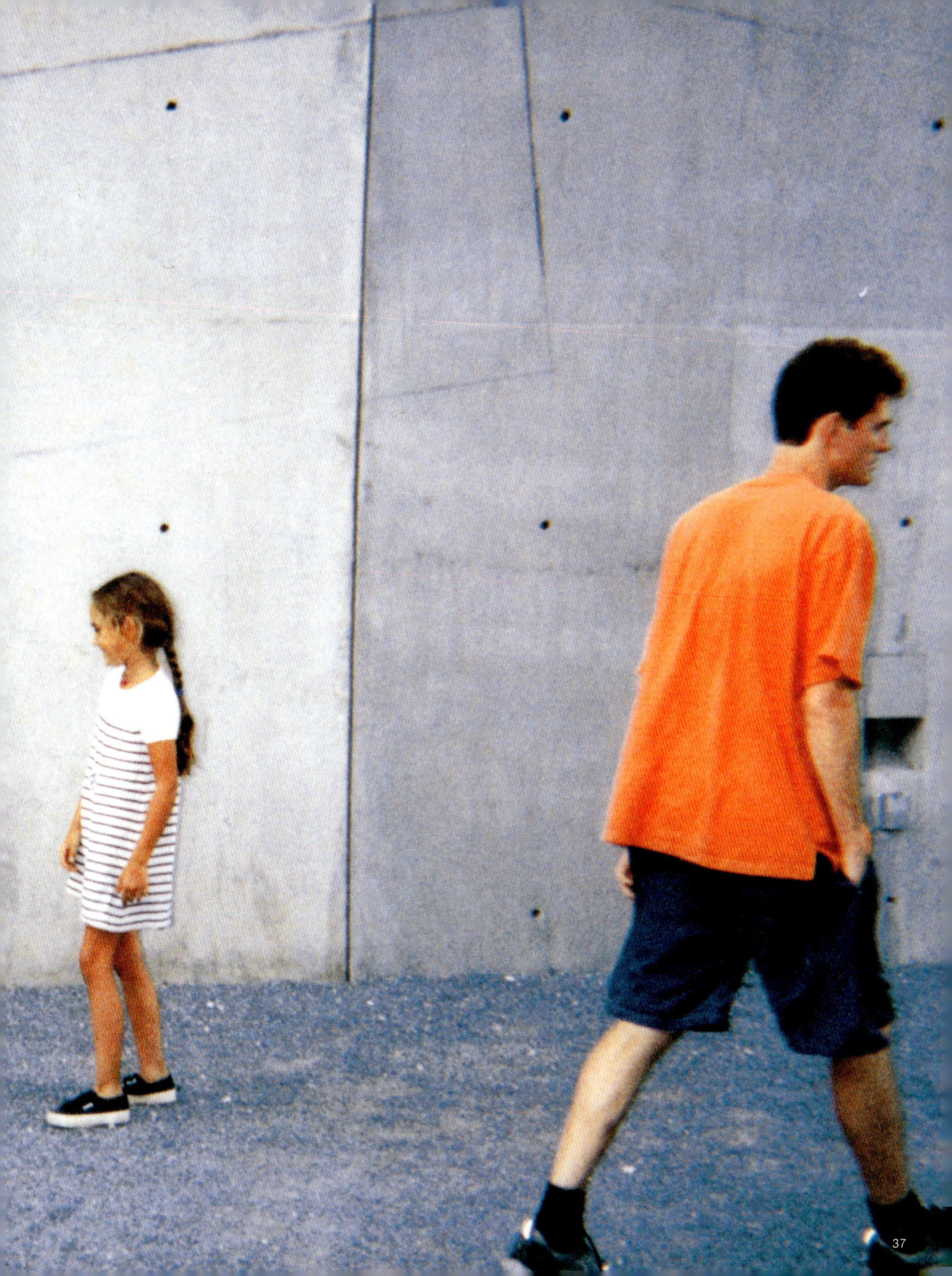

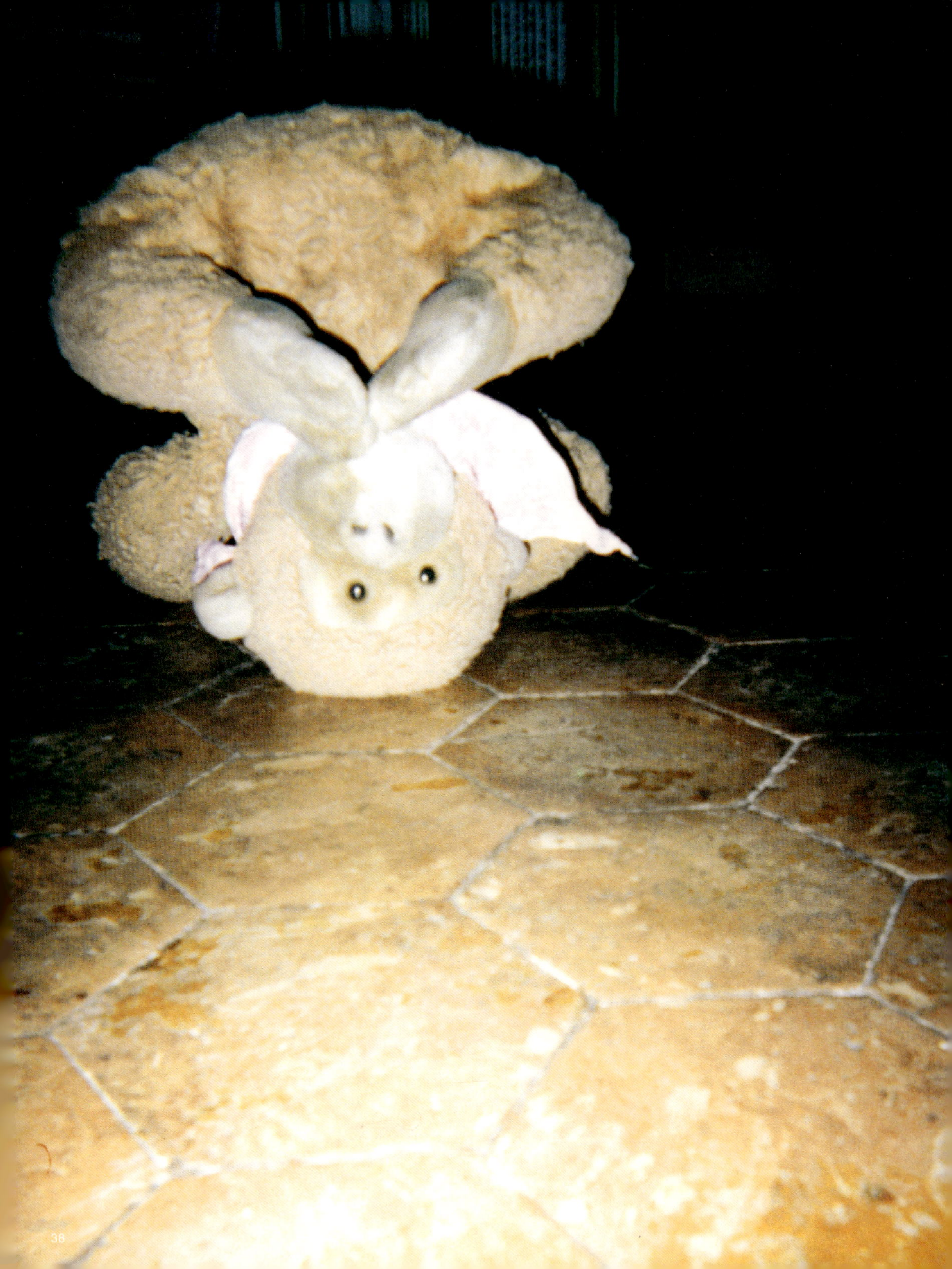

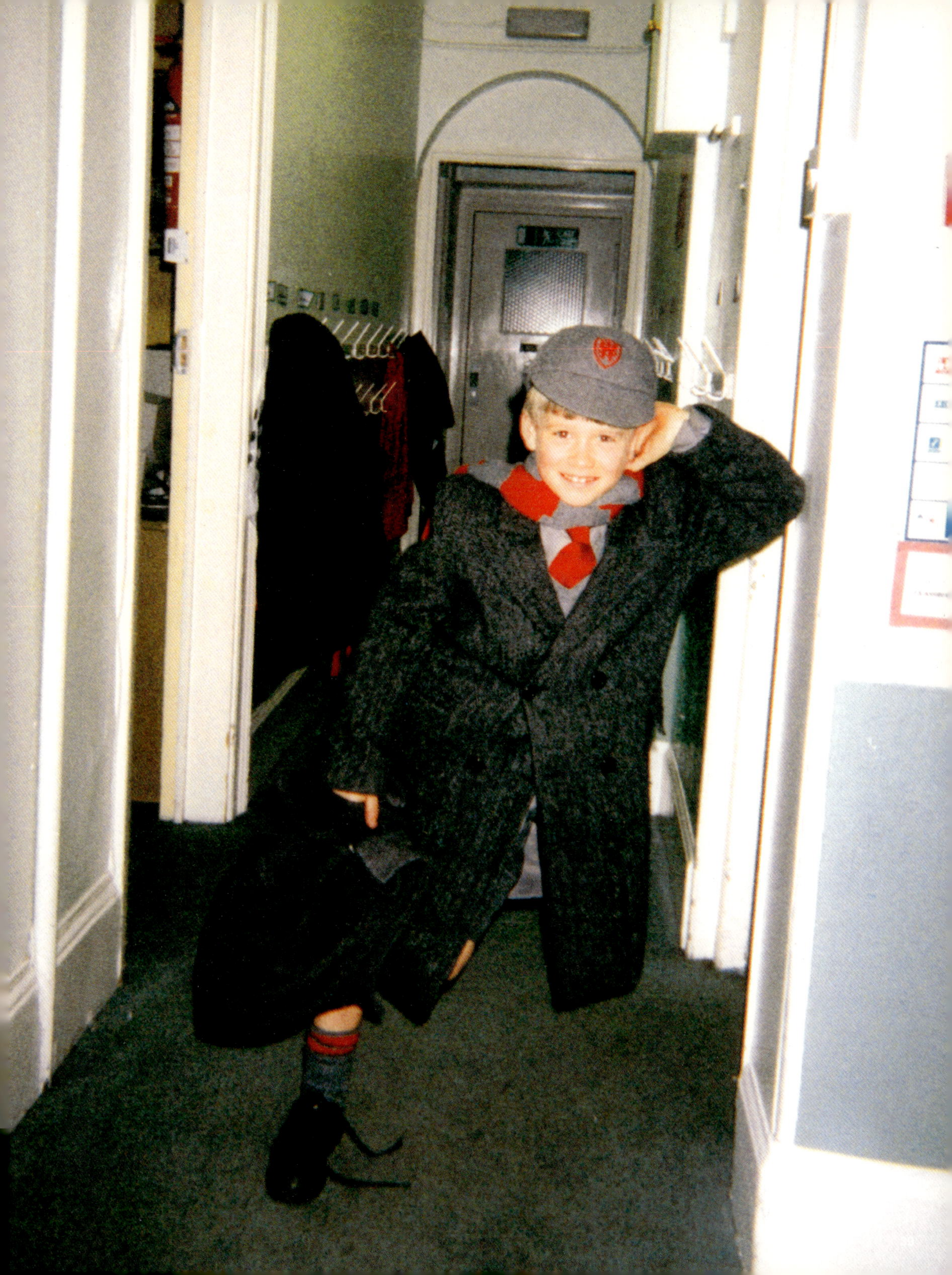

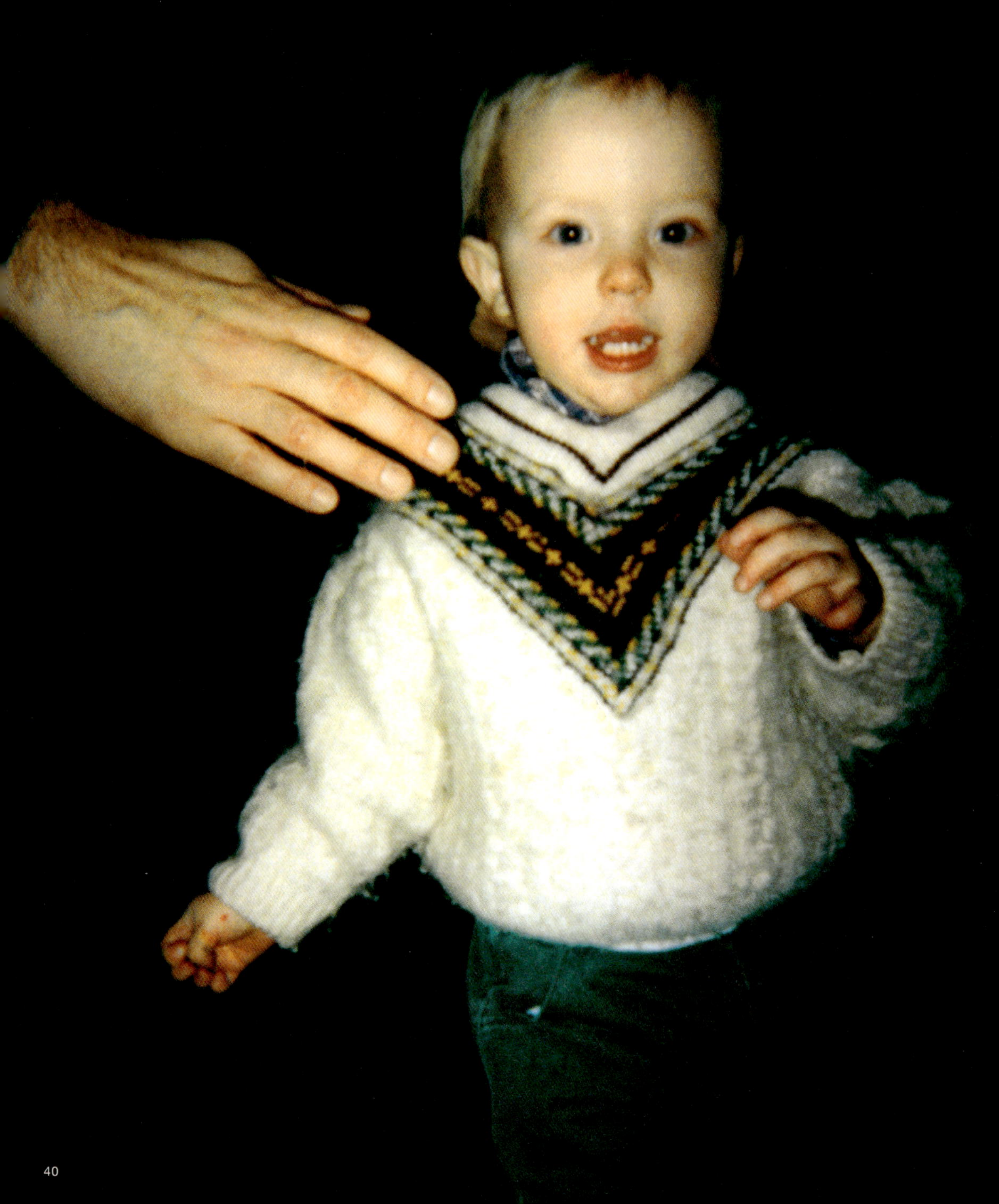

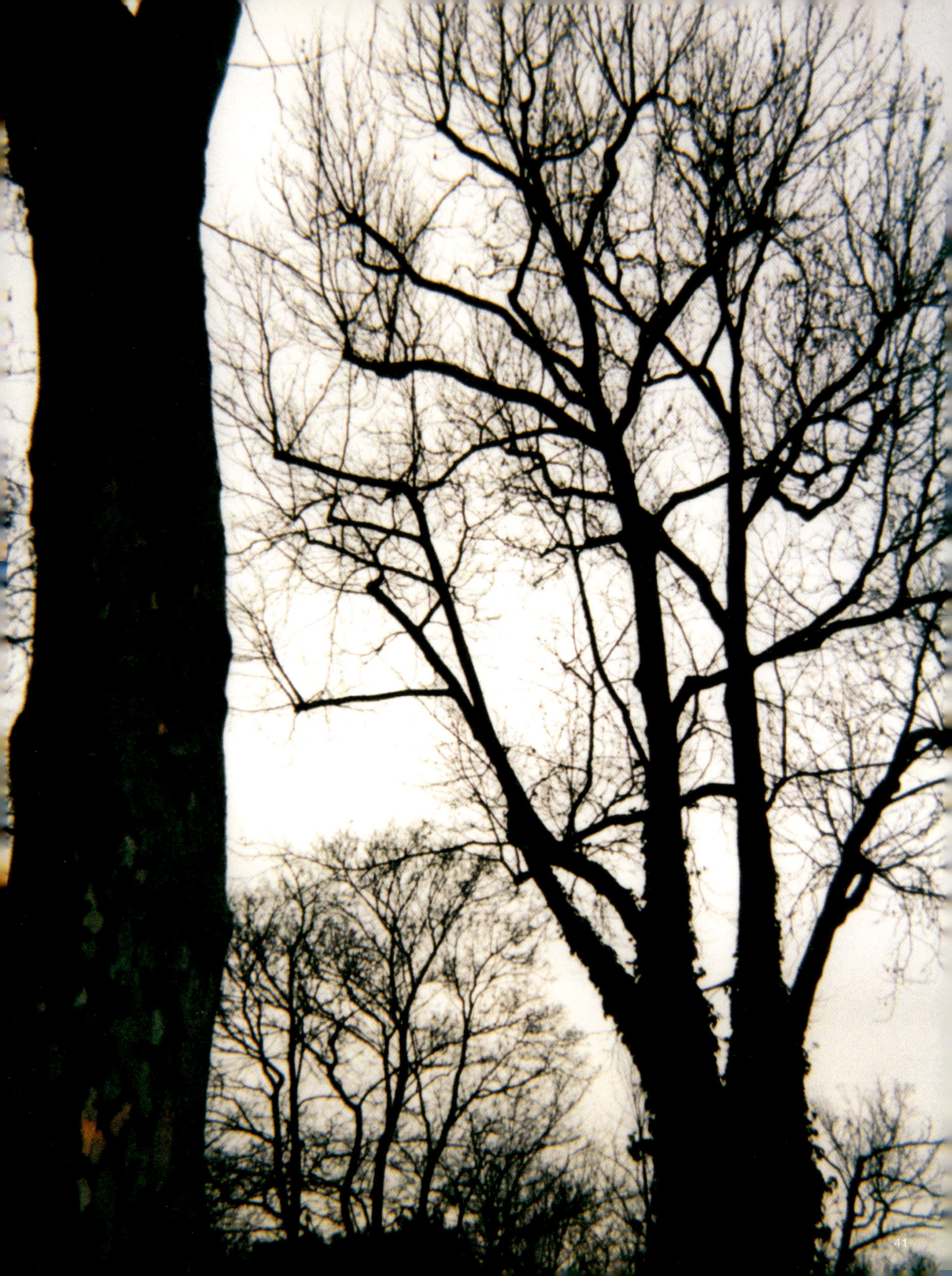

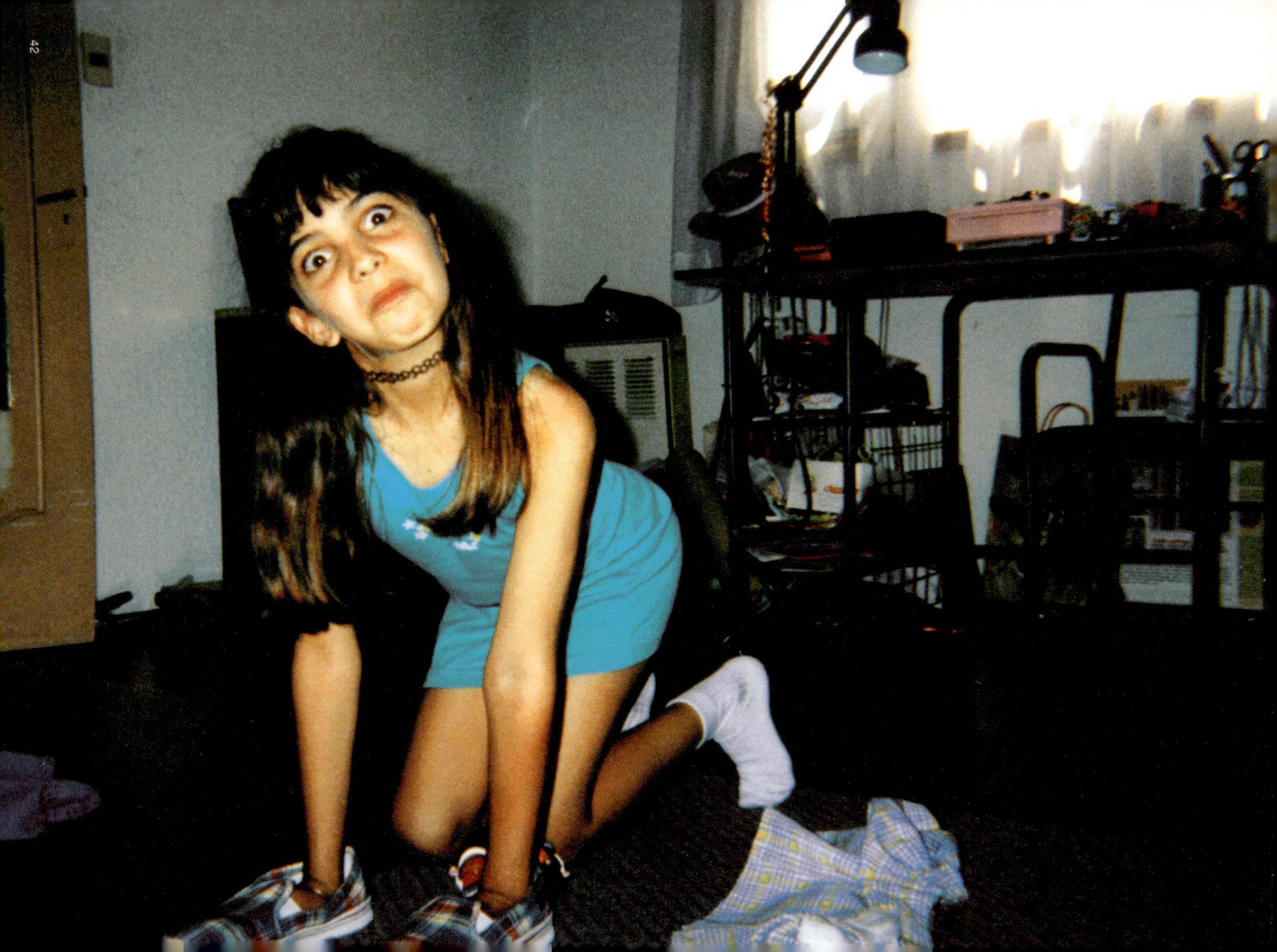

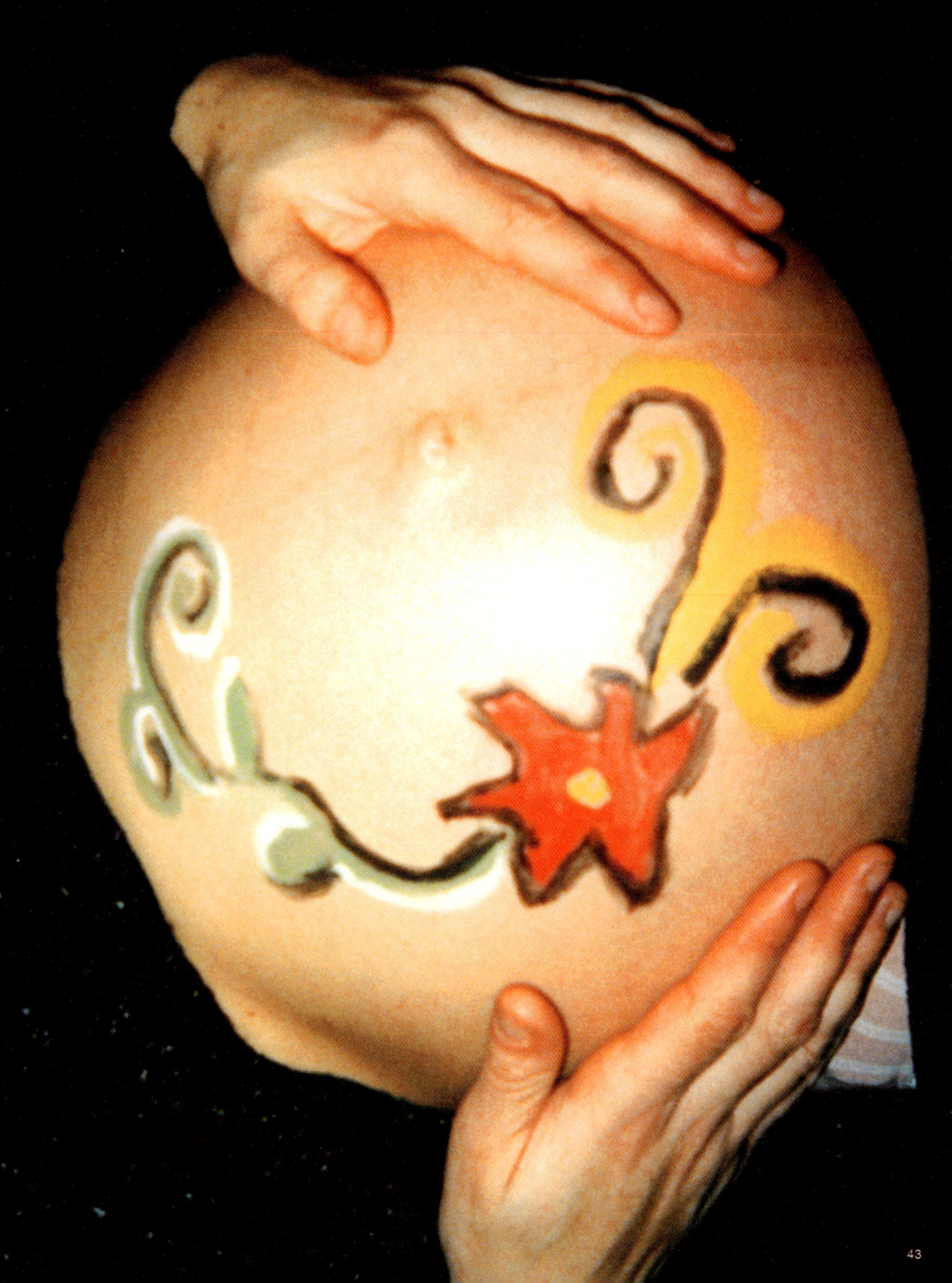

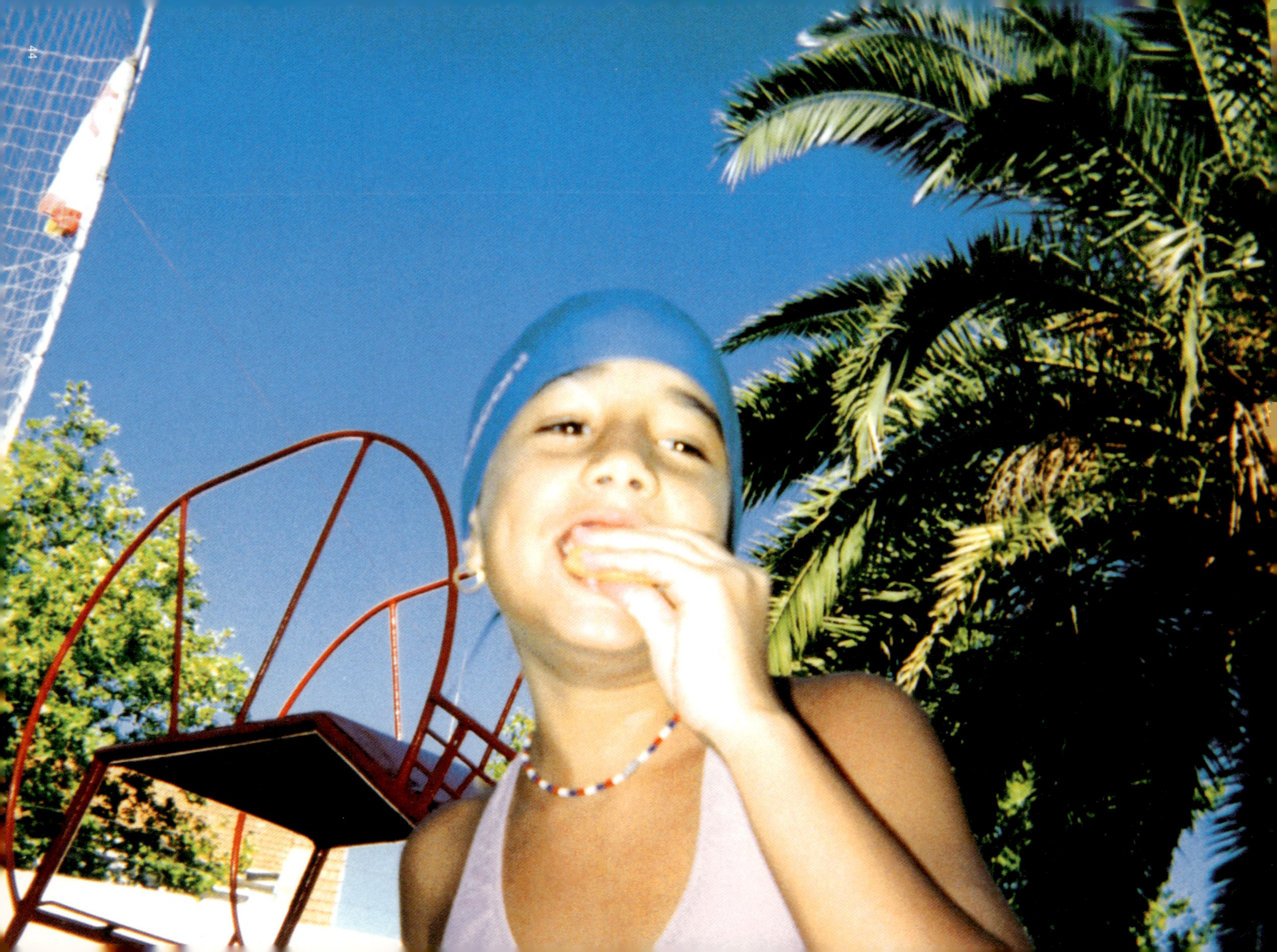

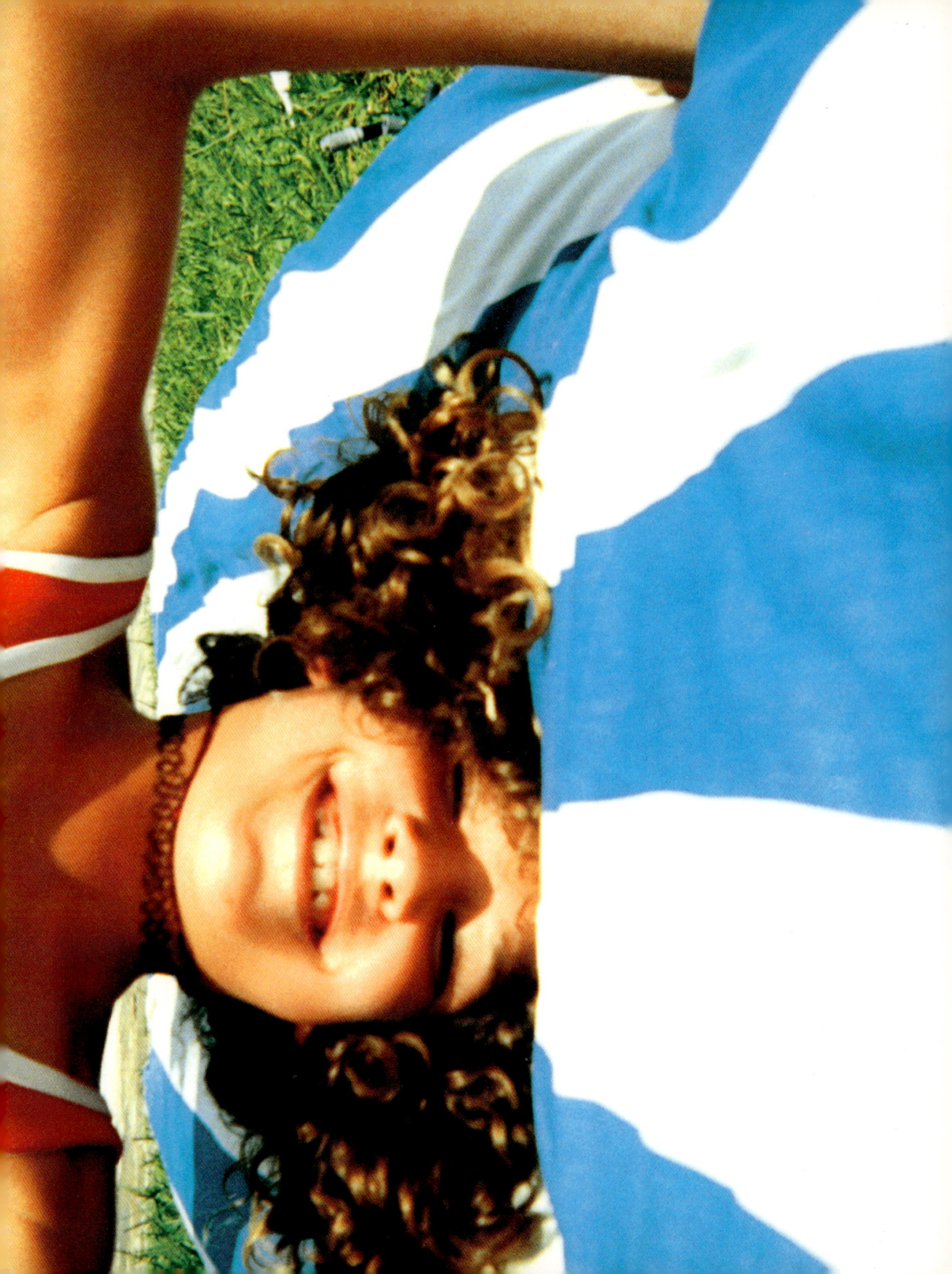

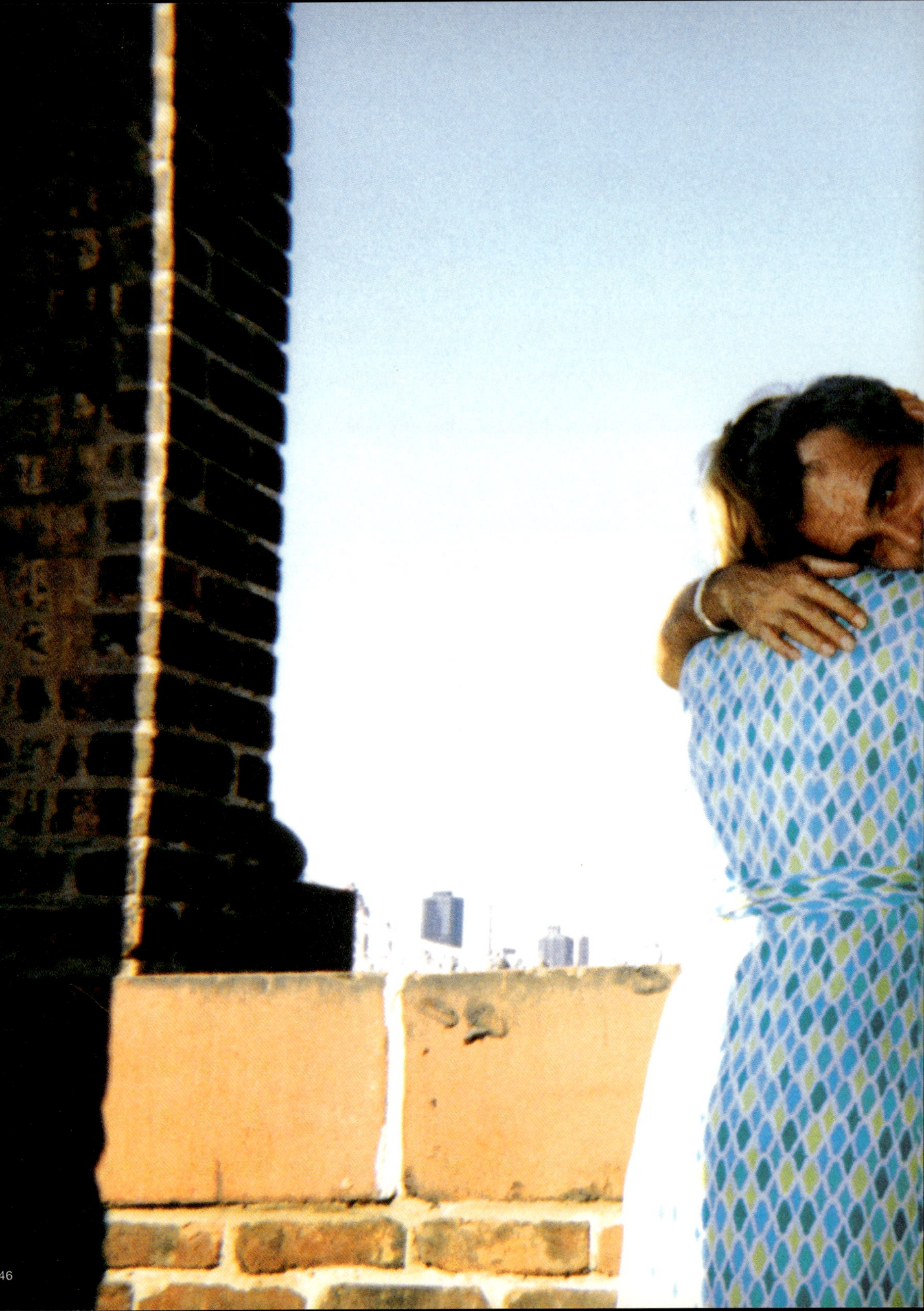

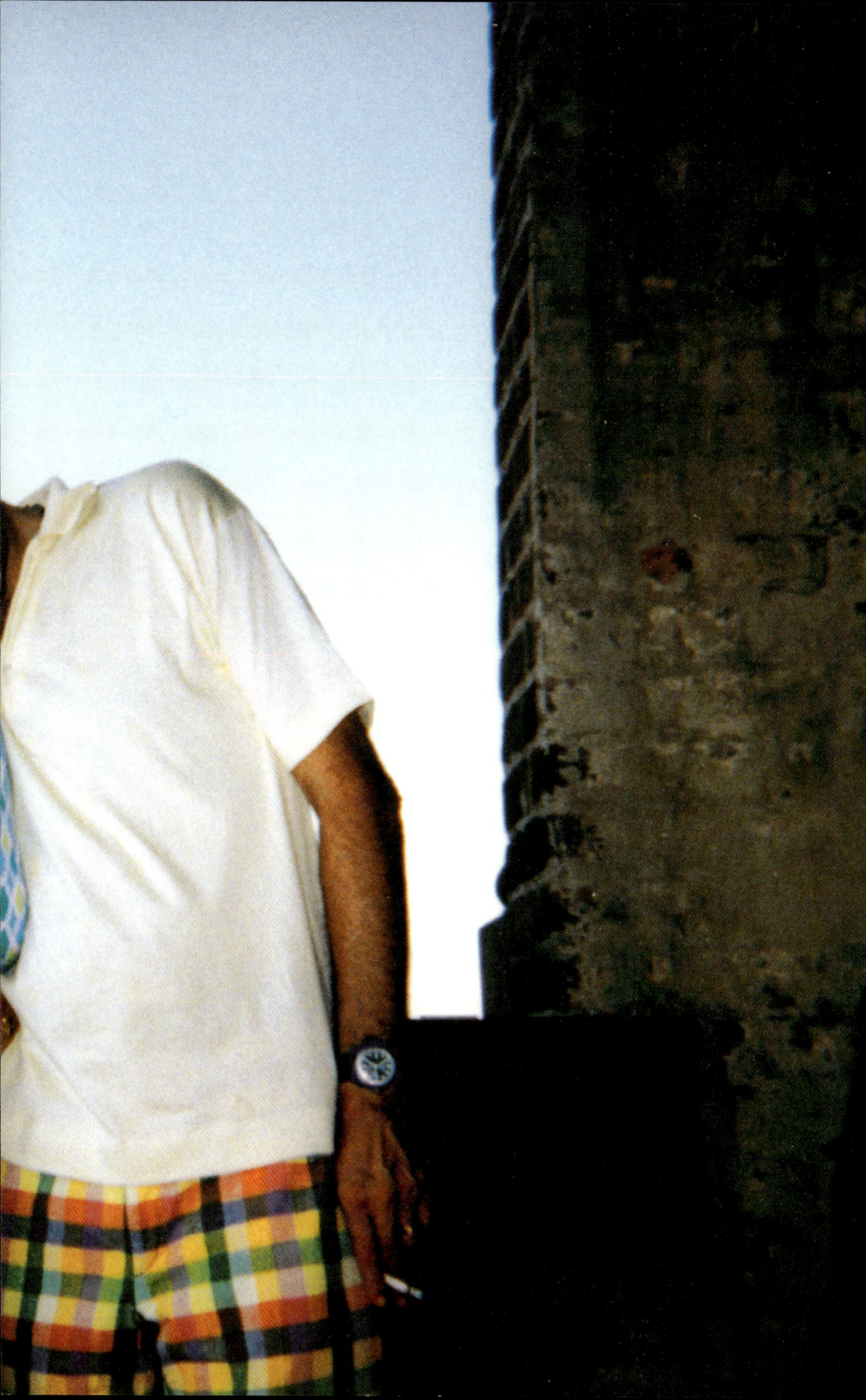

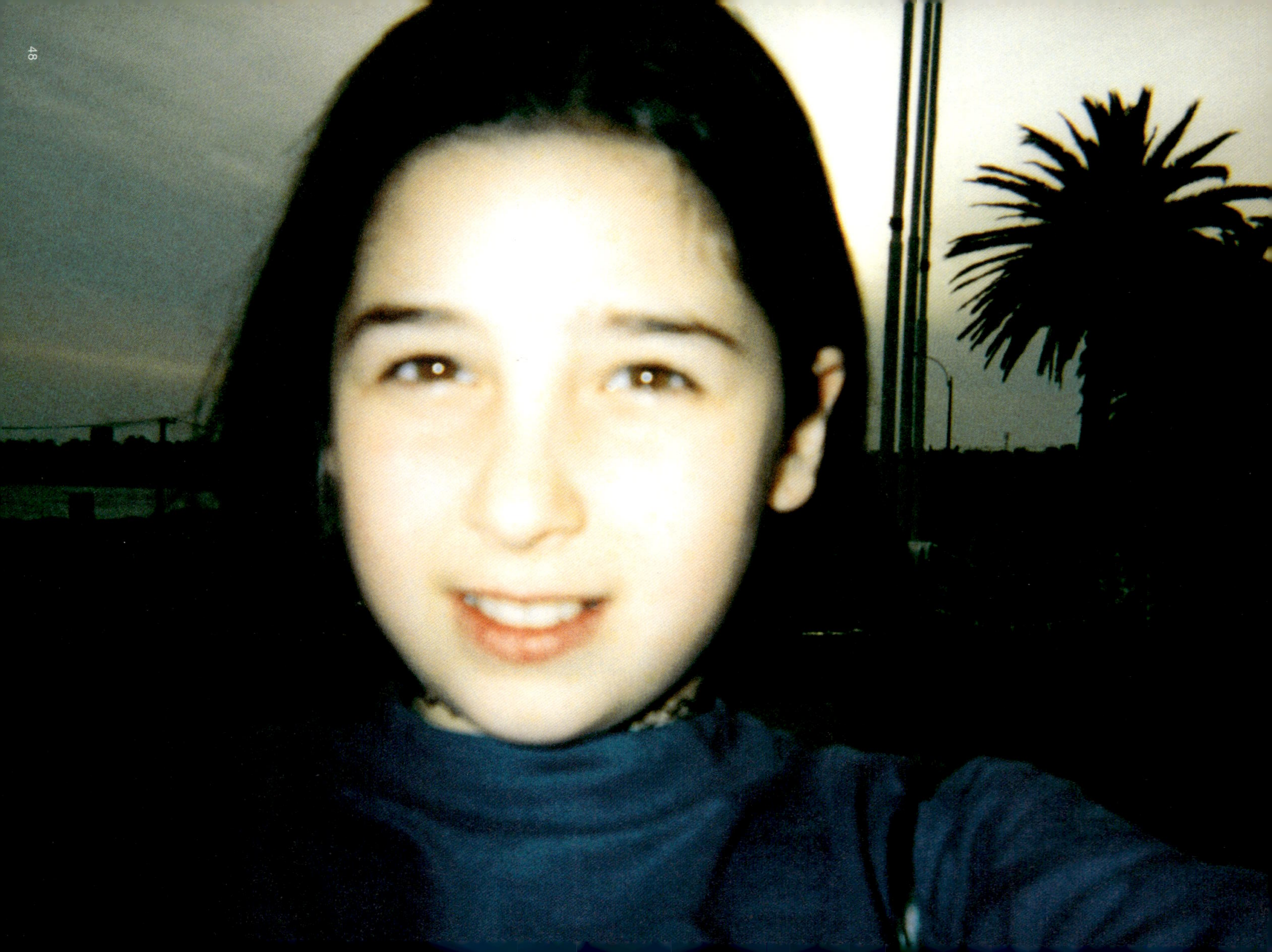

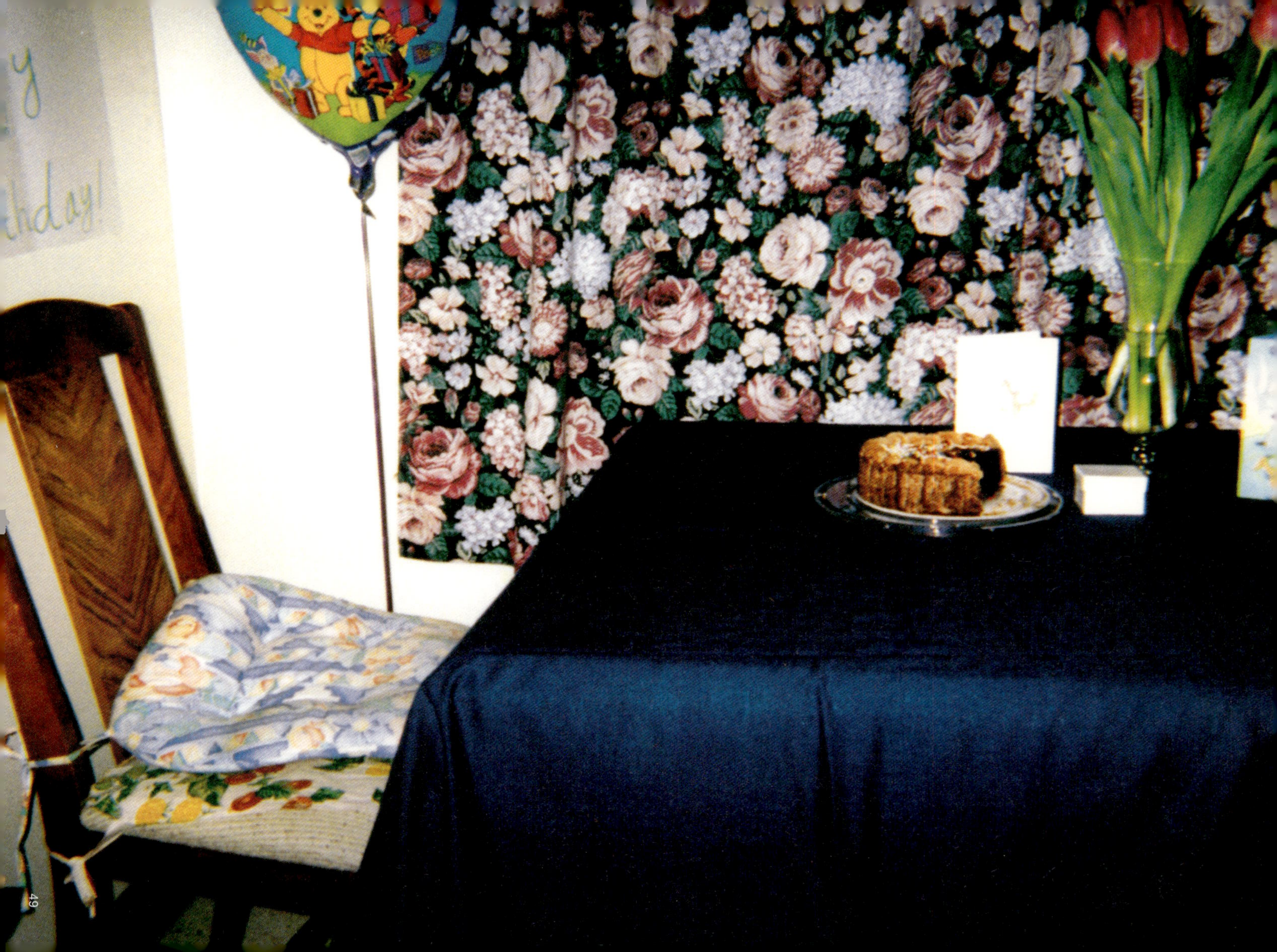

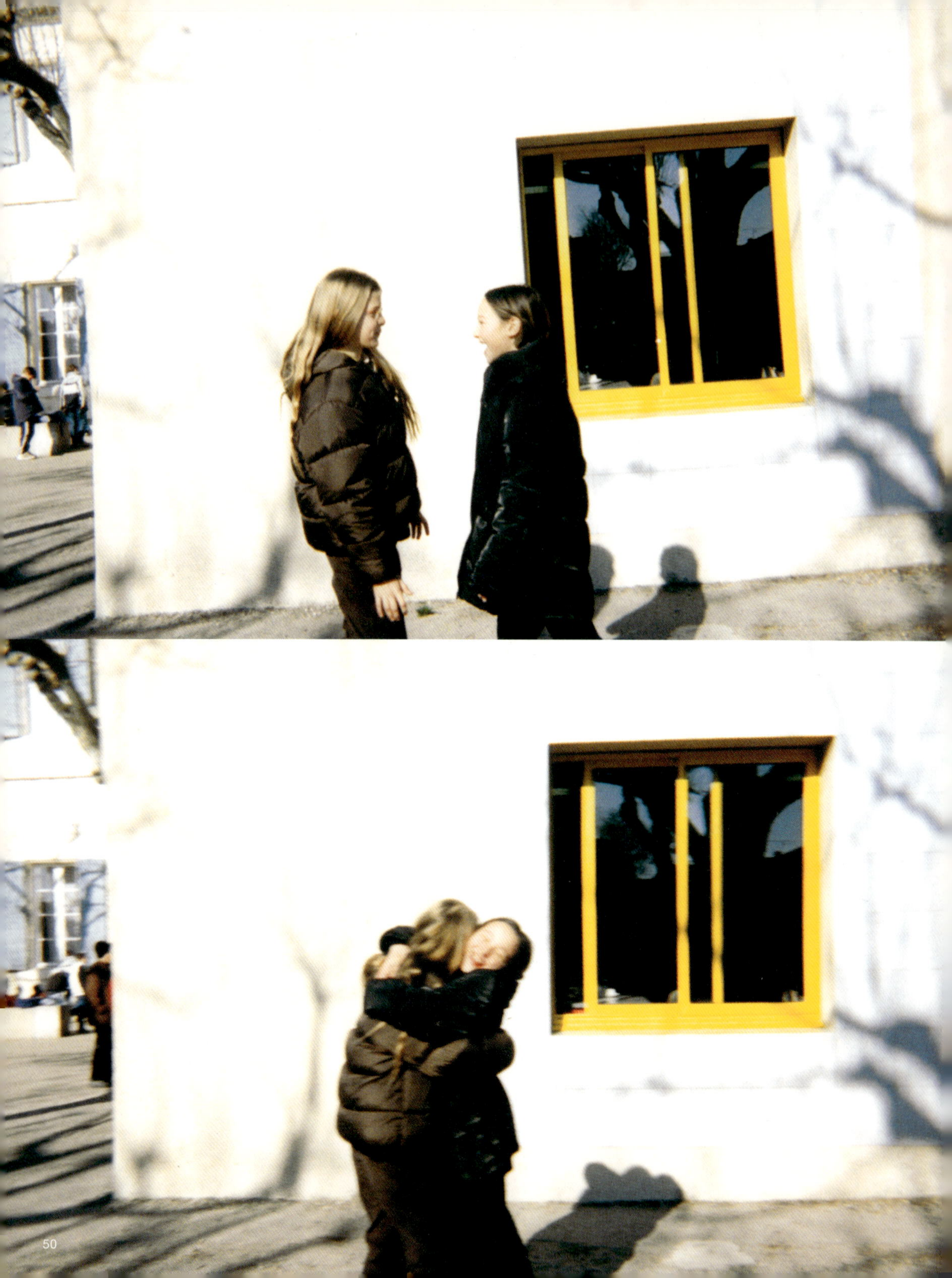

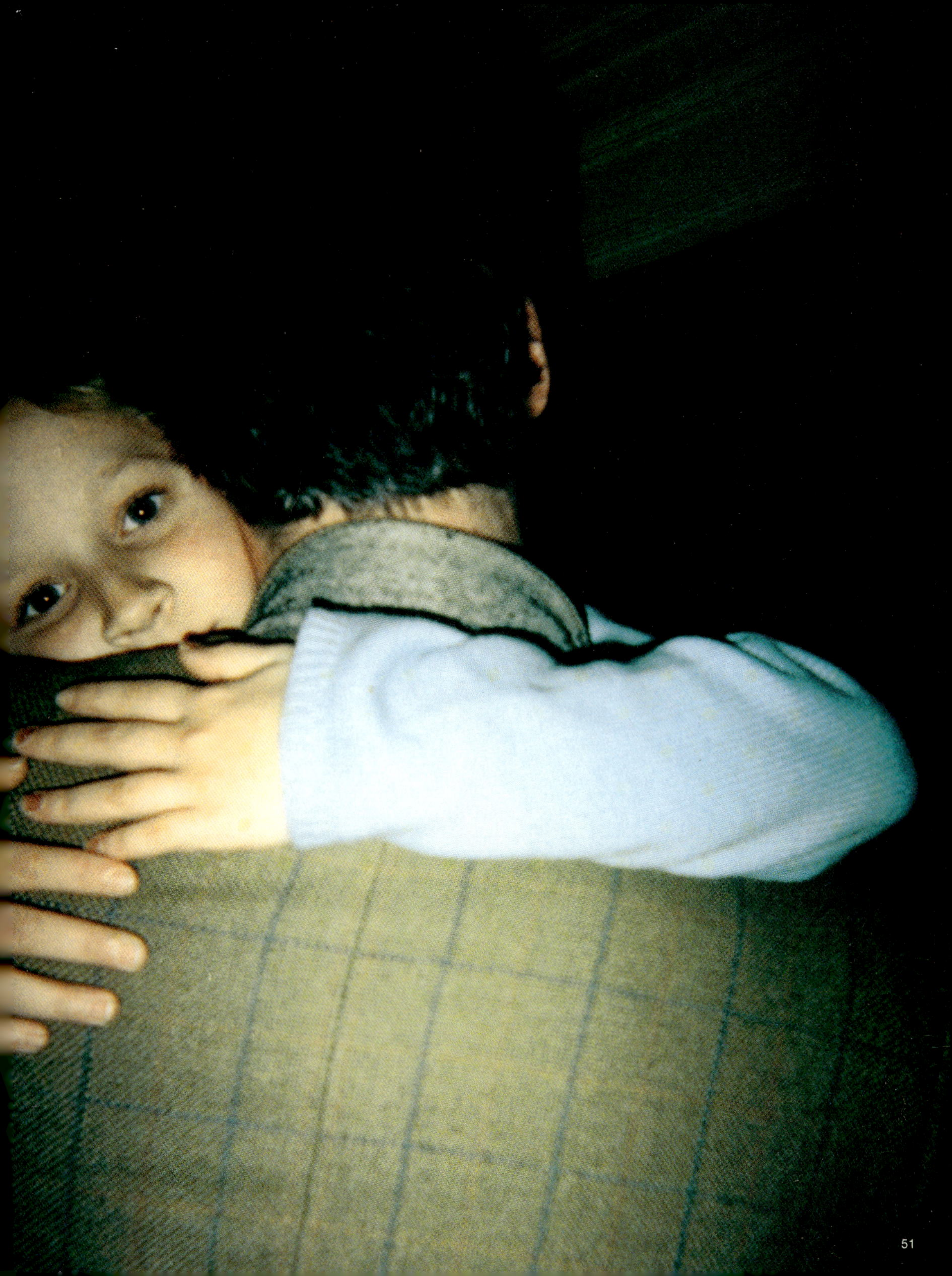

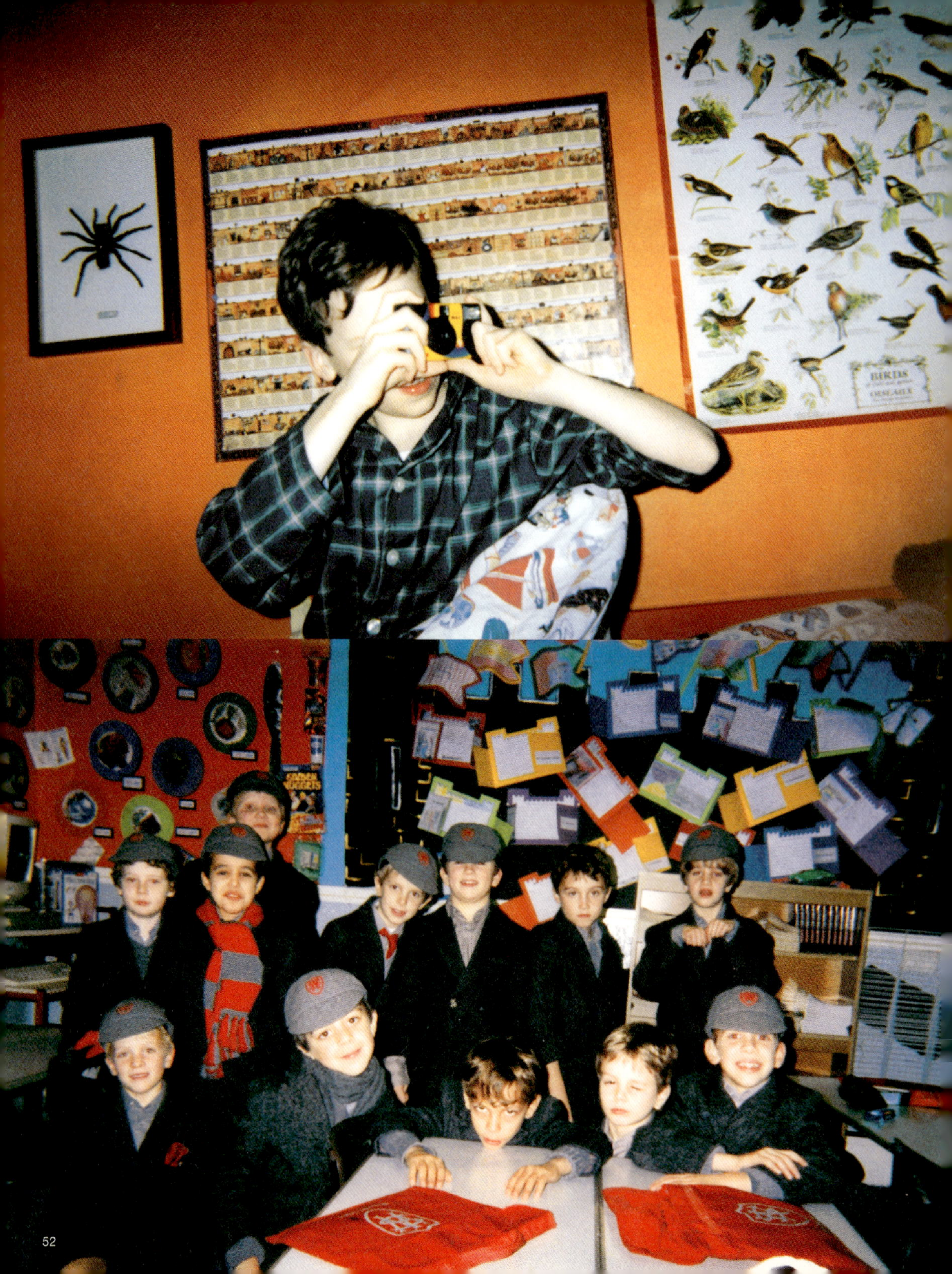

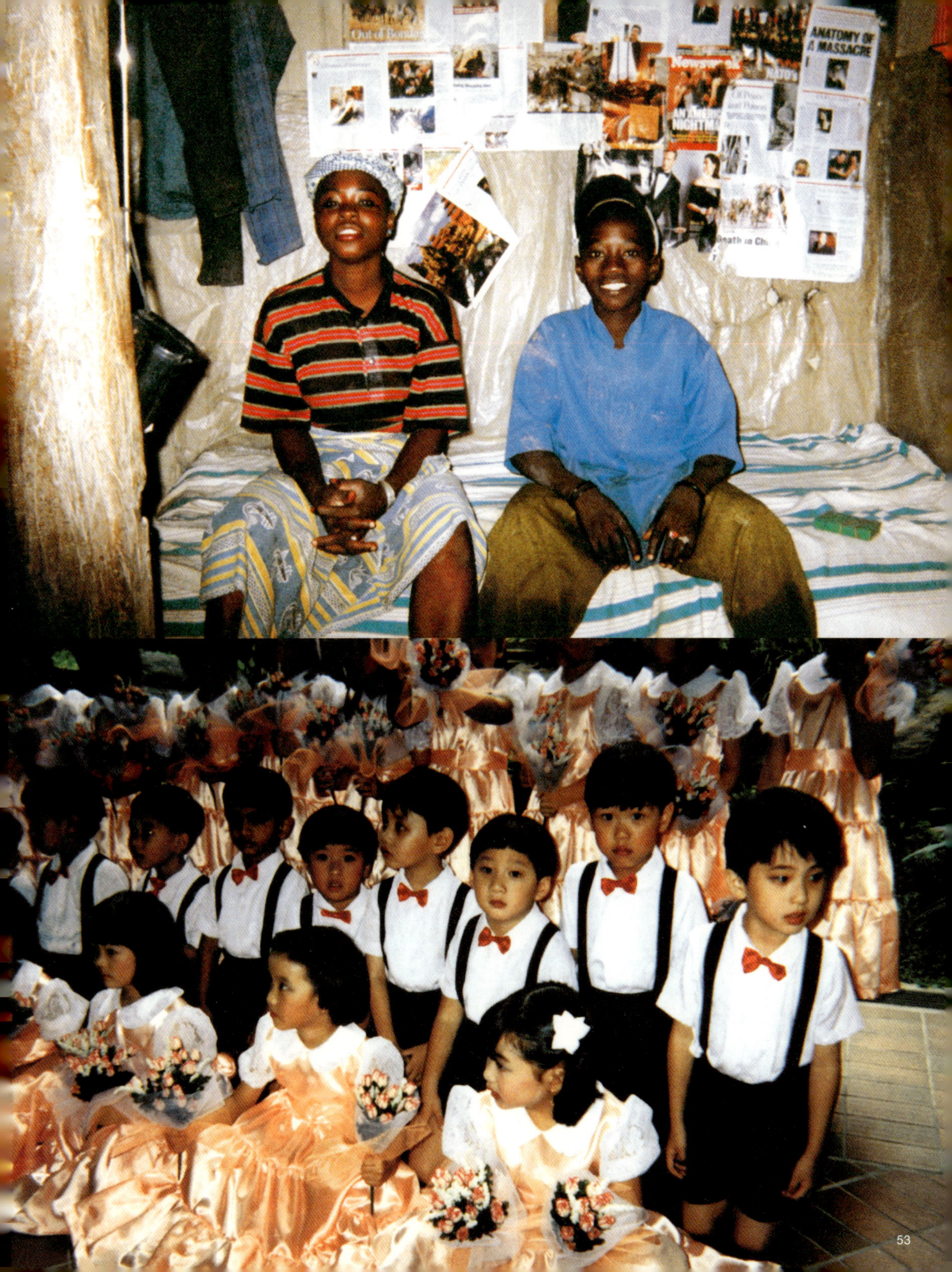

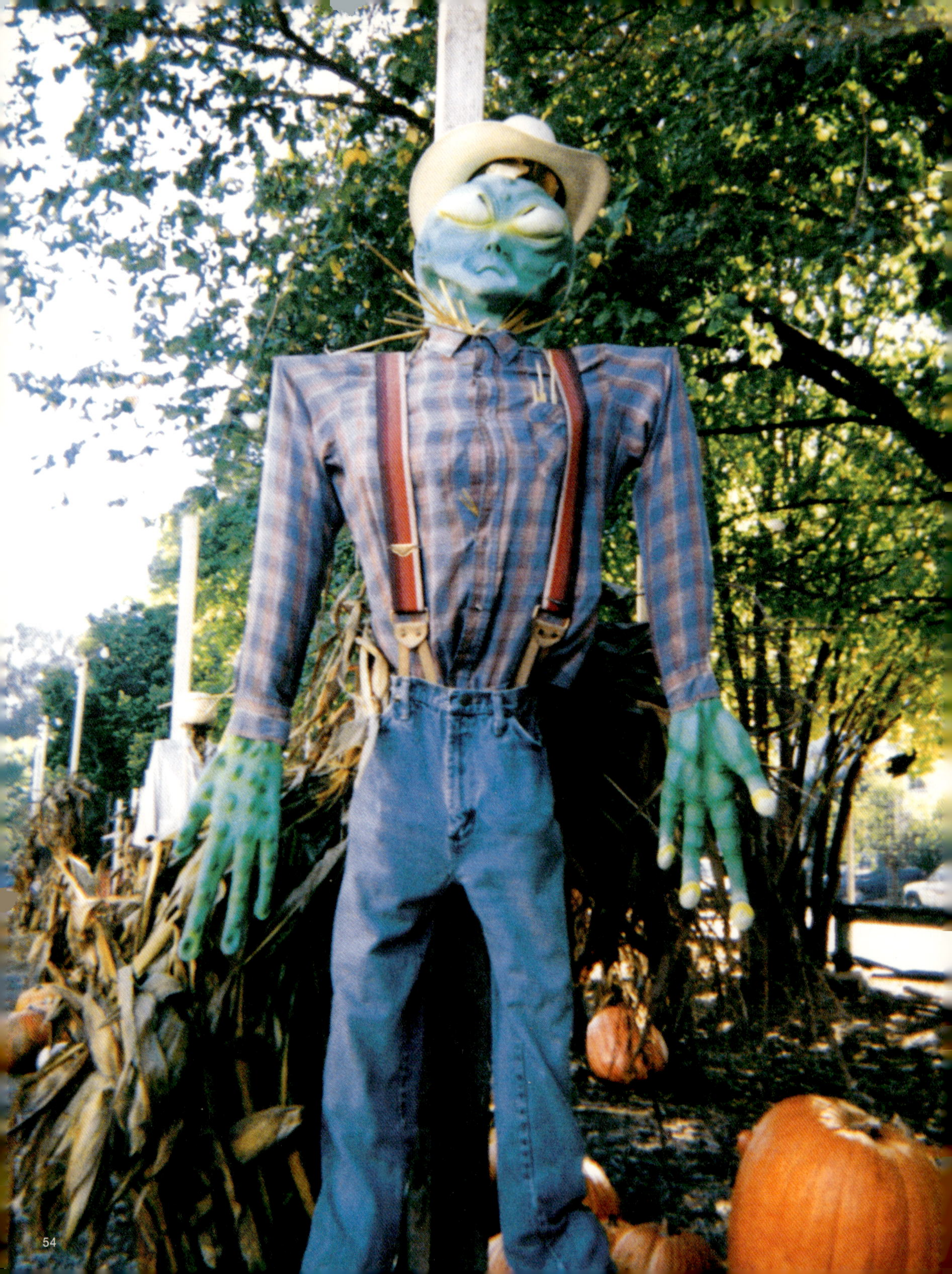

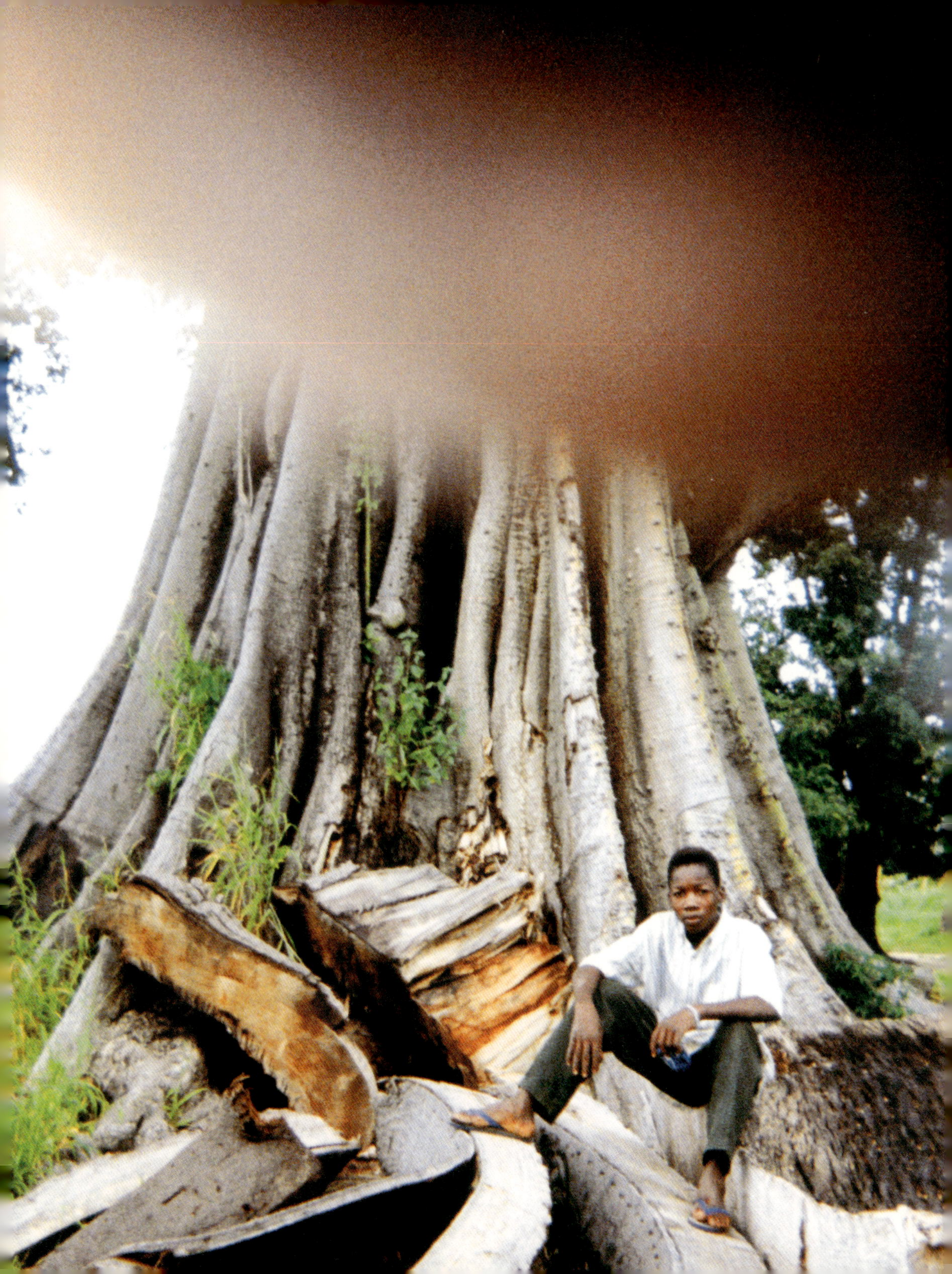

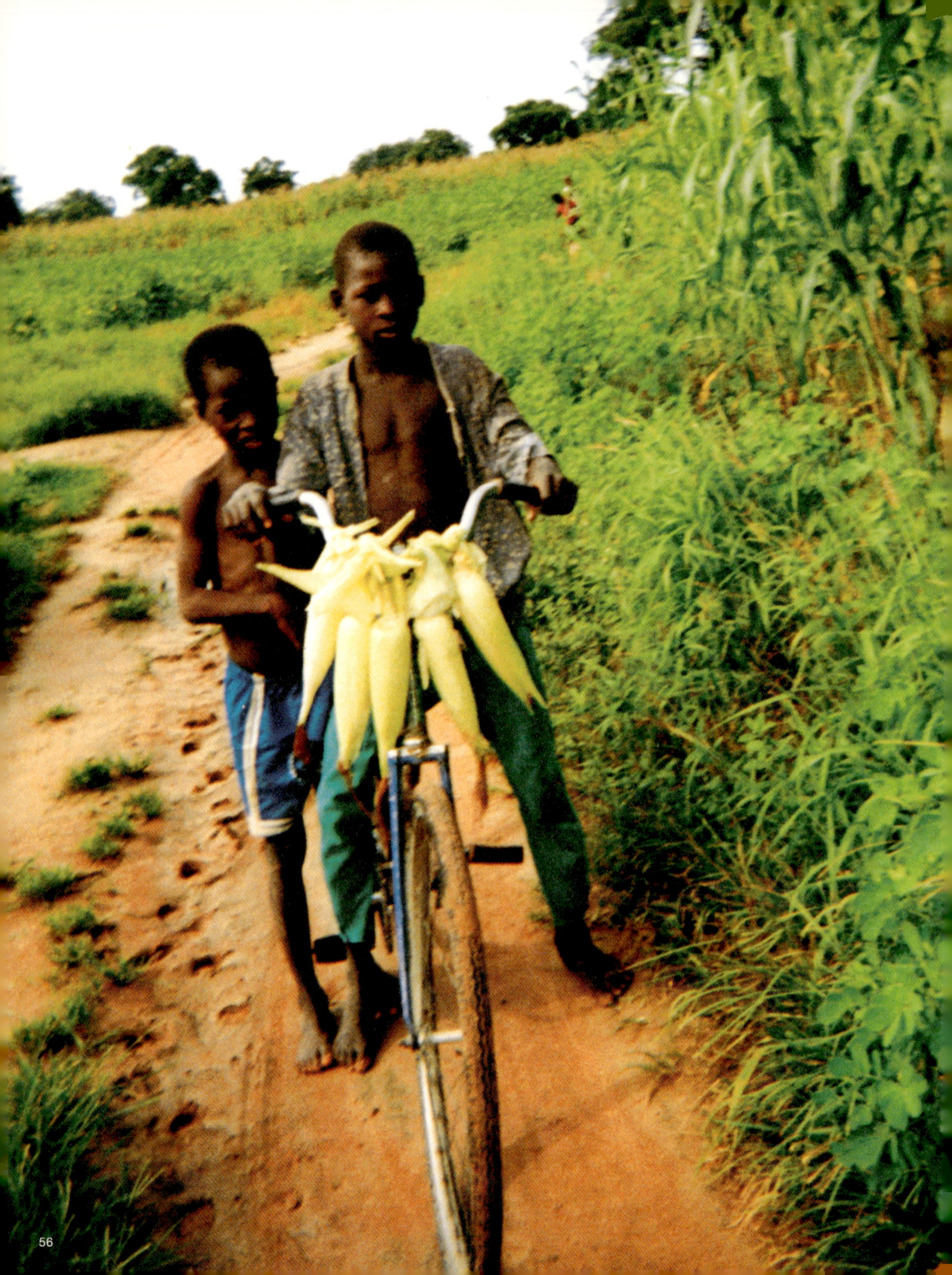

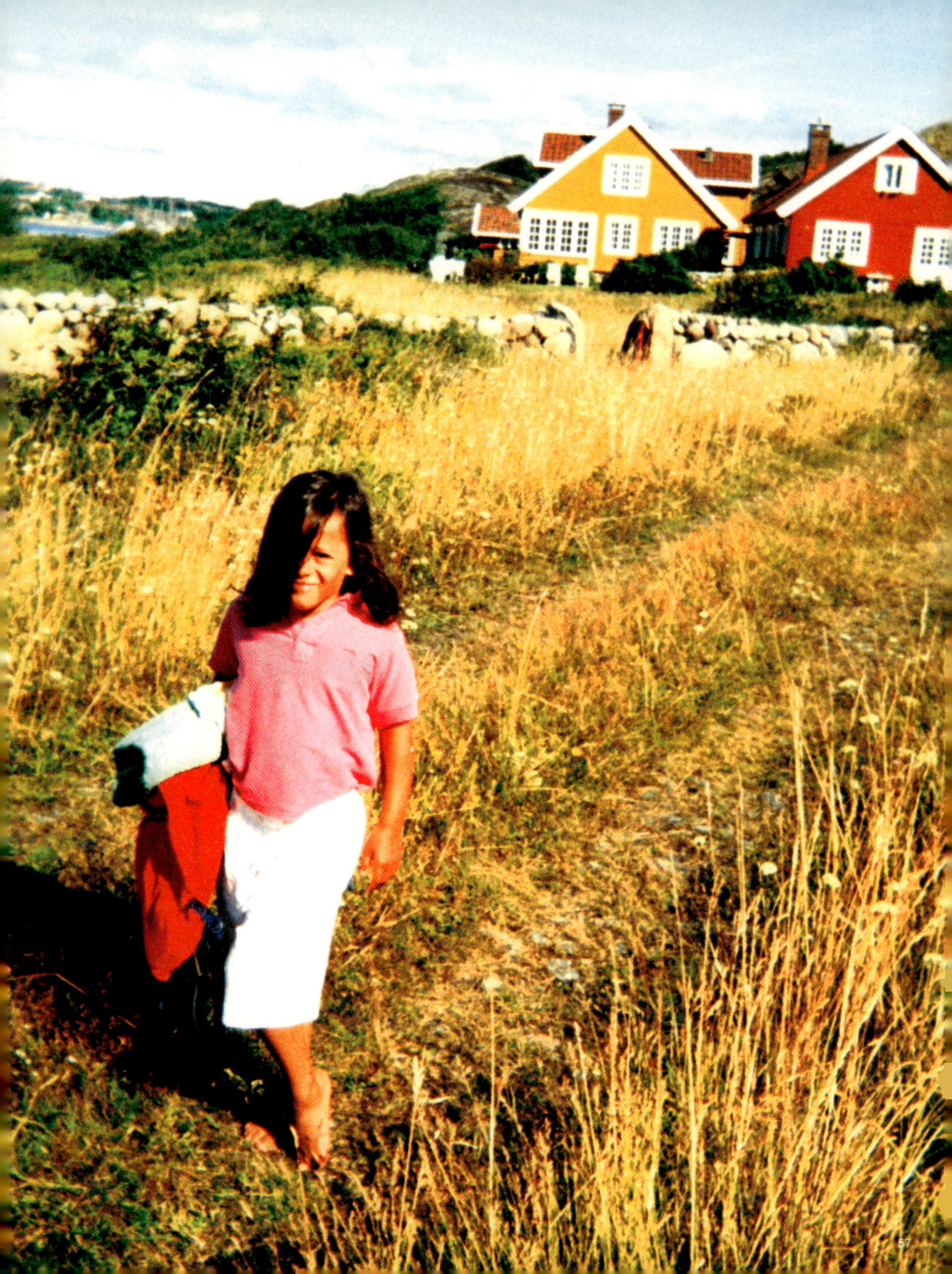

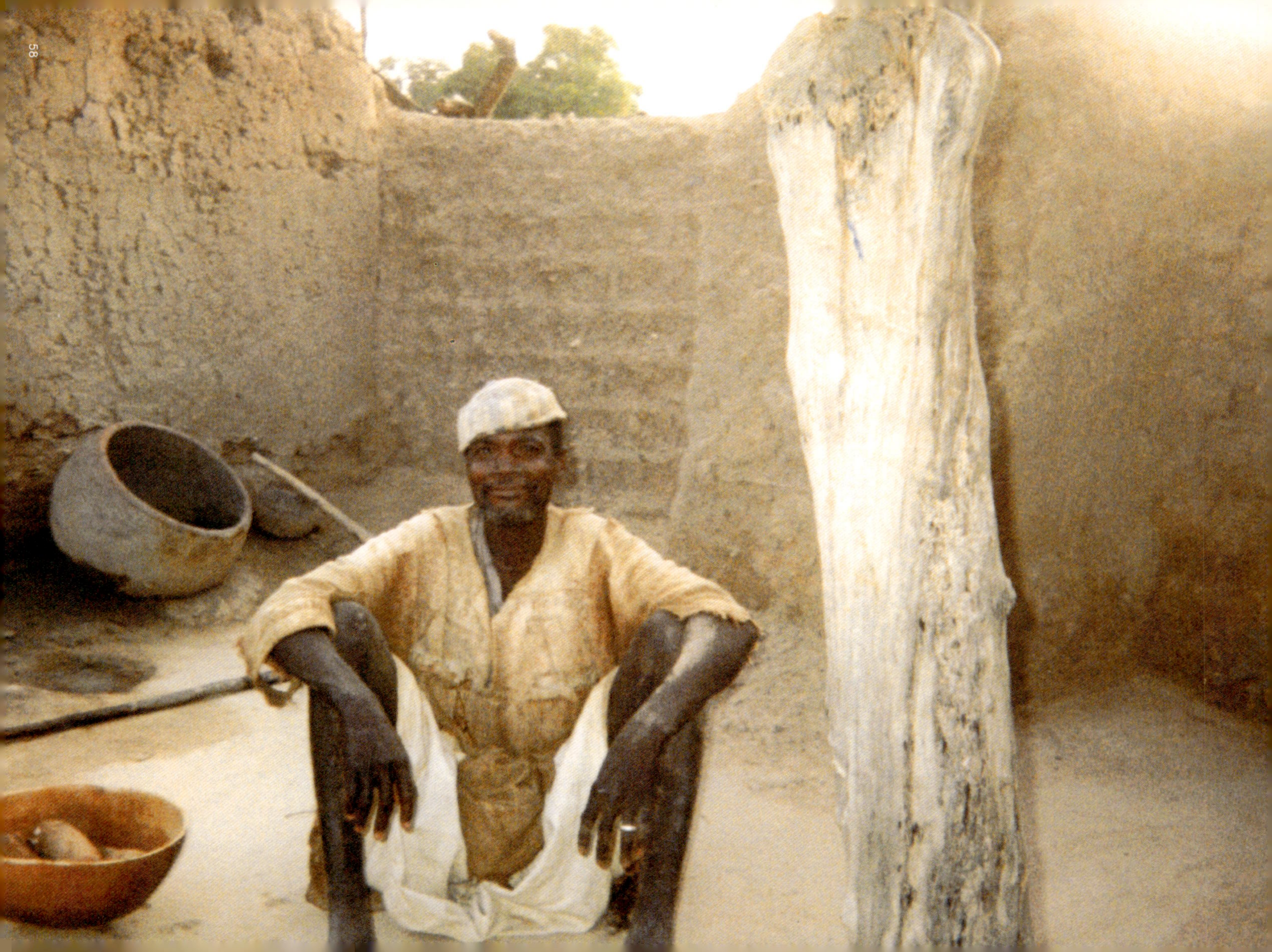

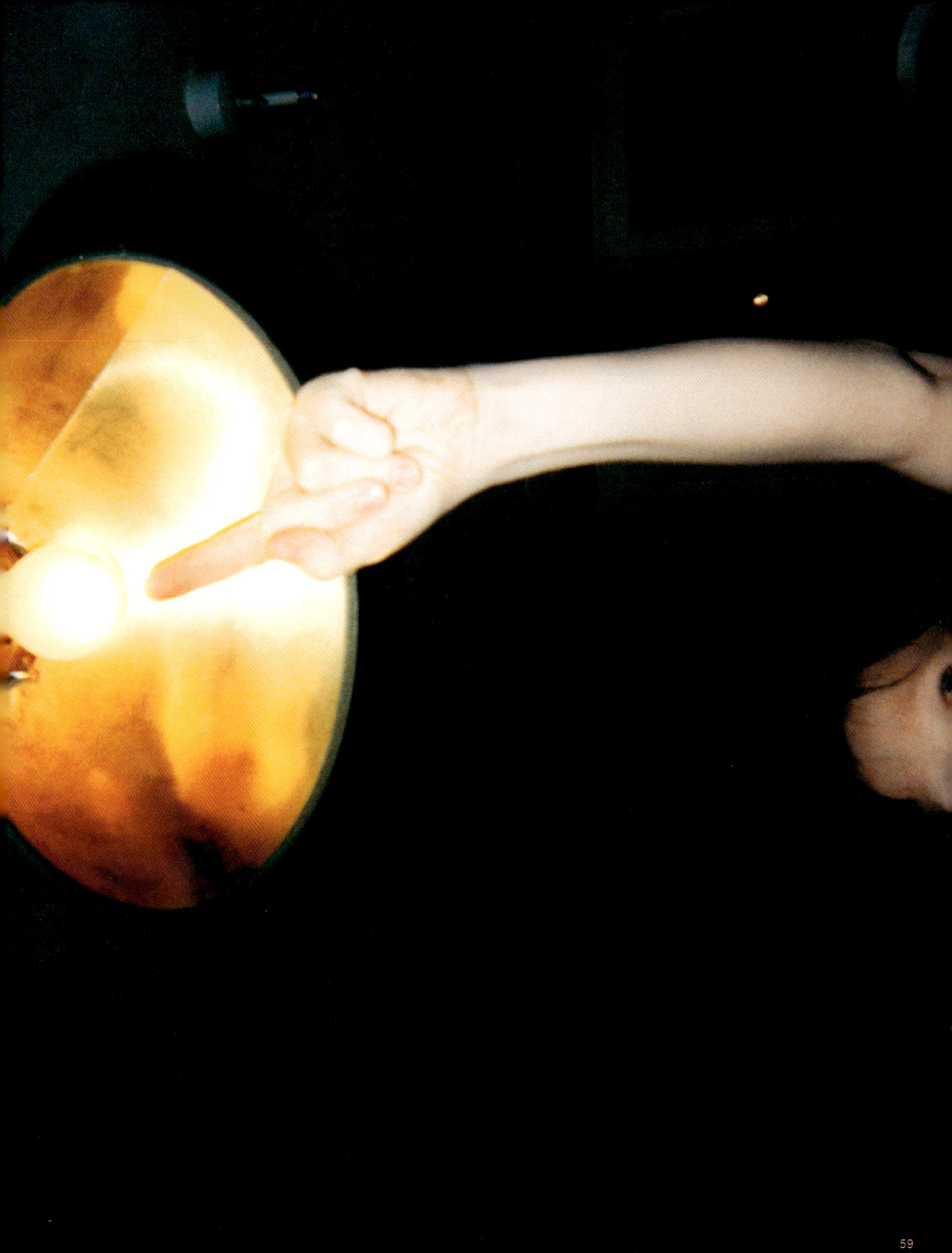

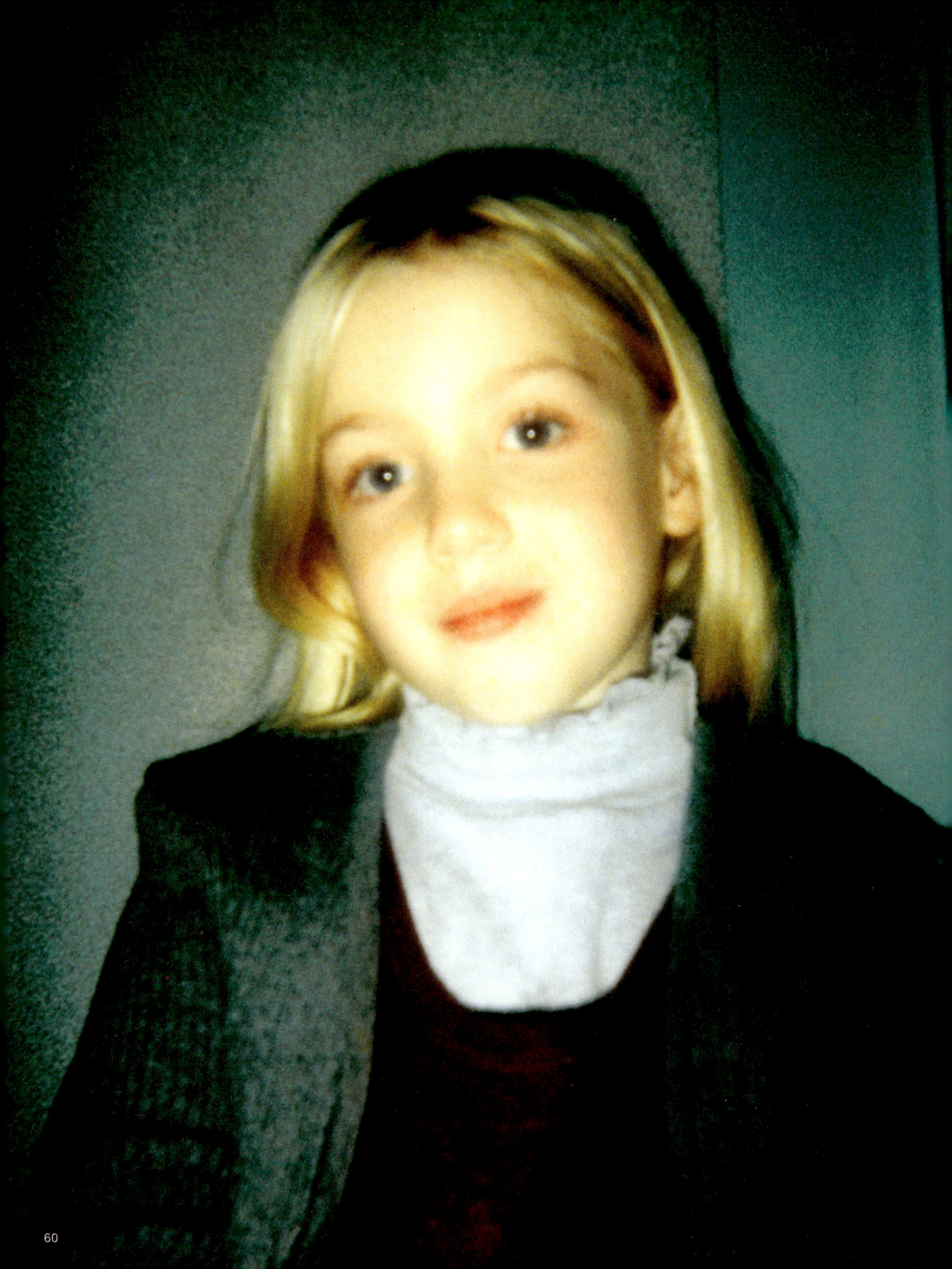

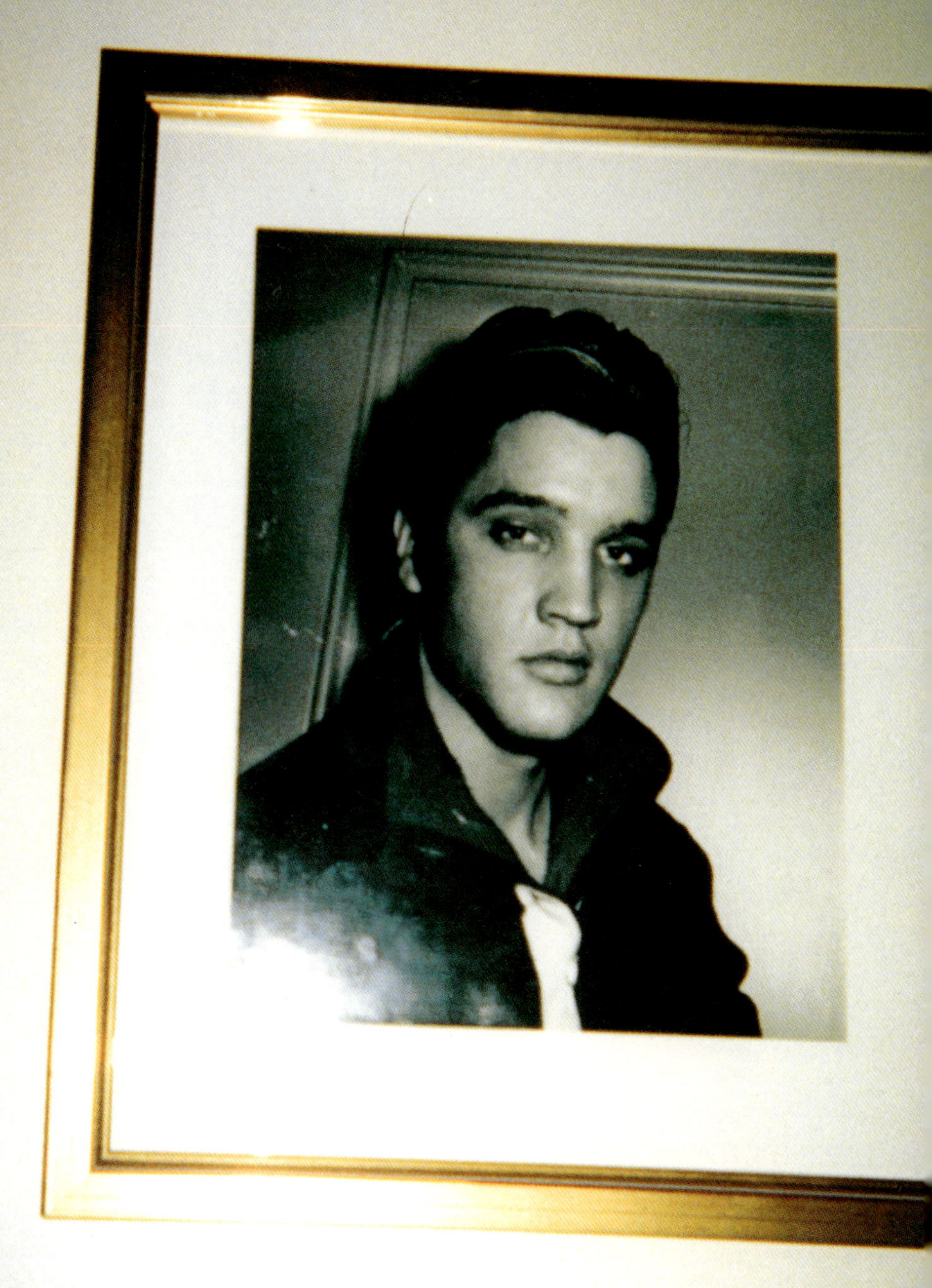

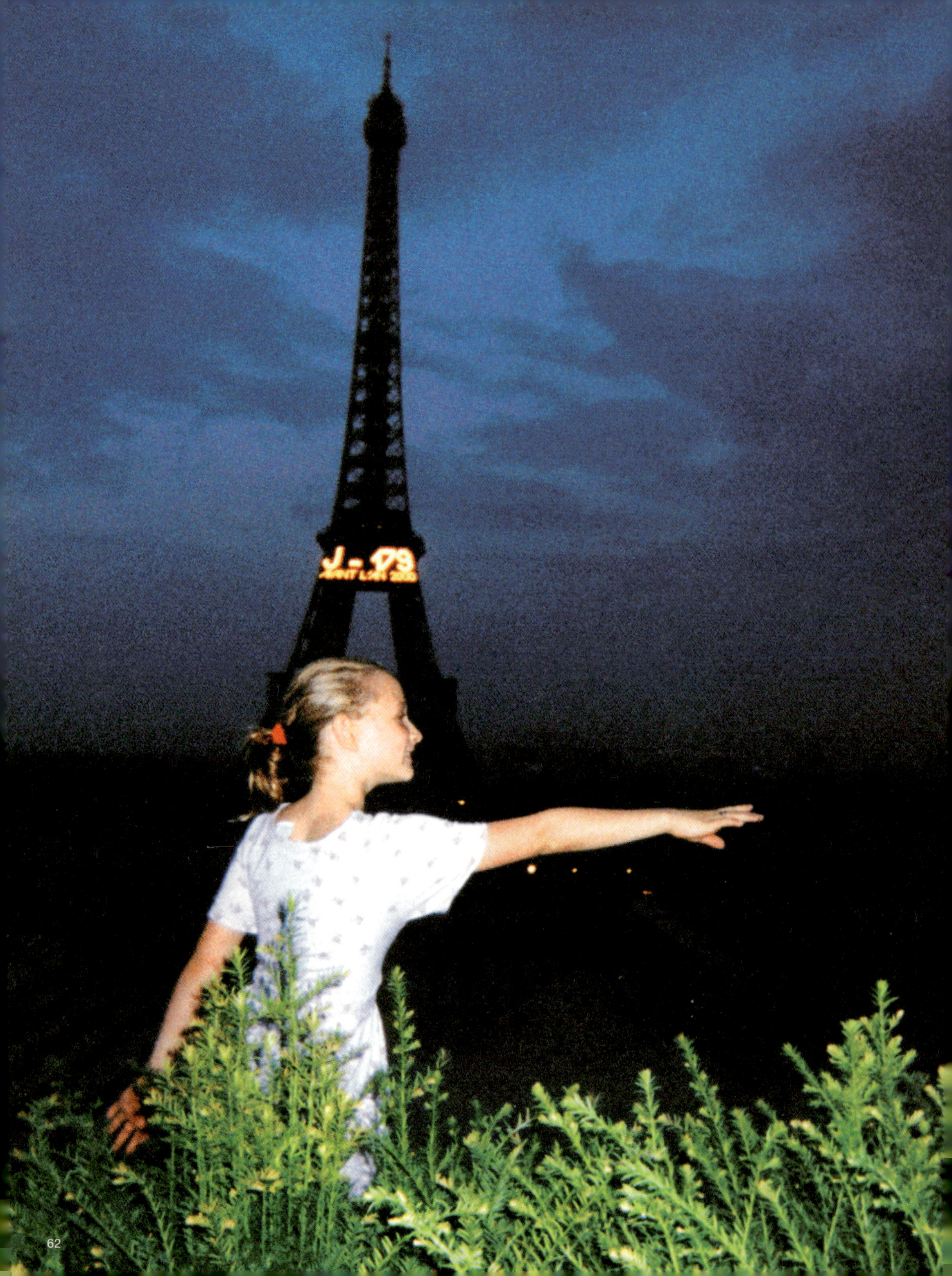
J - 179
AVANT L'AN 2000

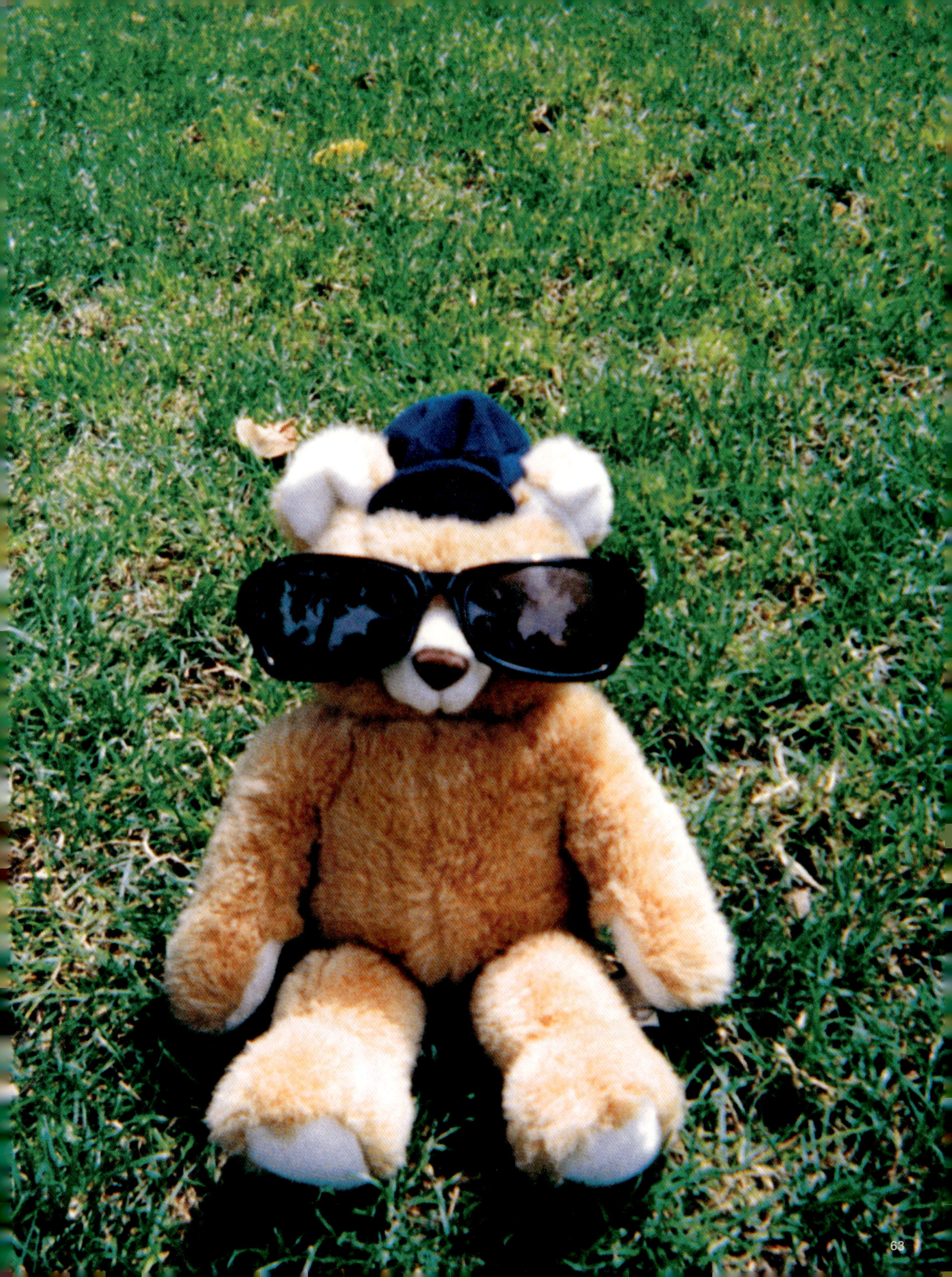

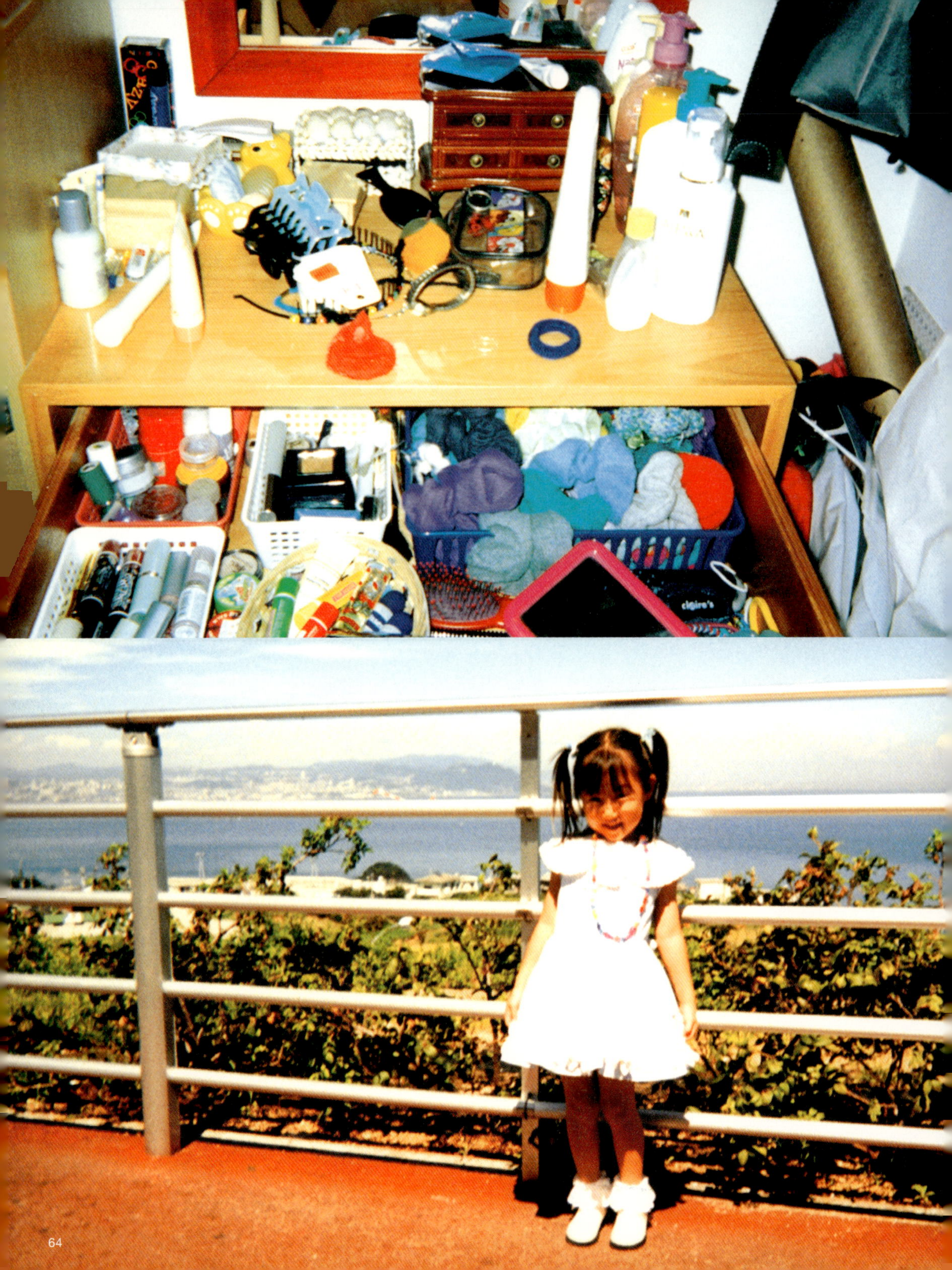

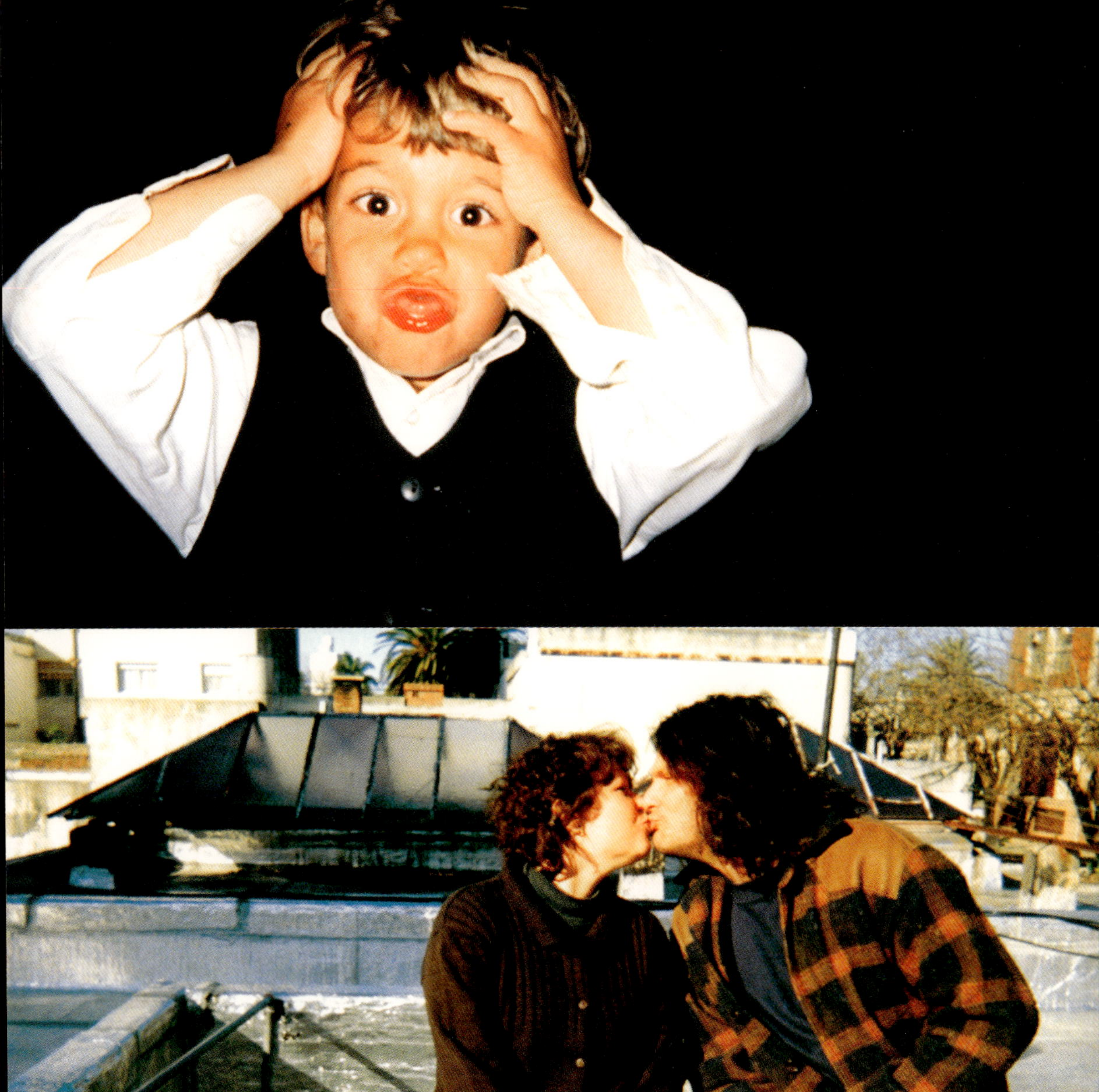

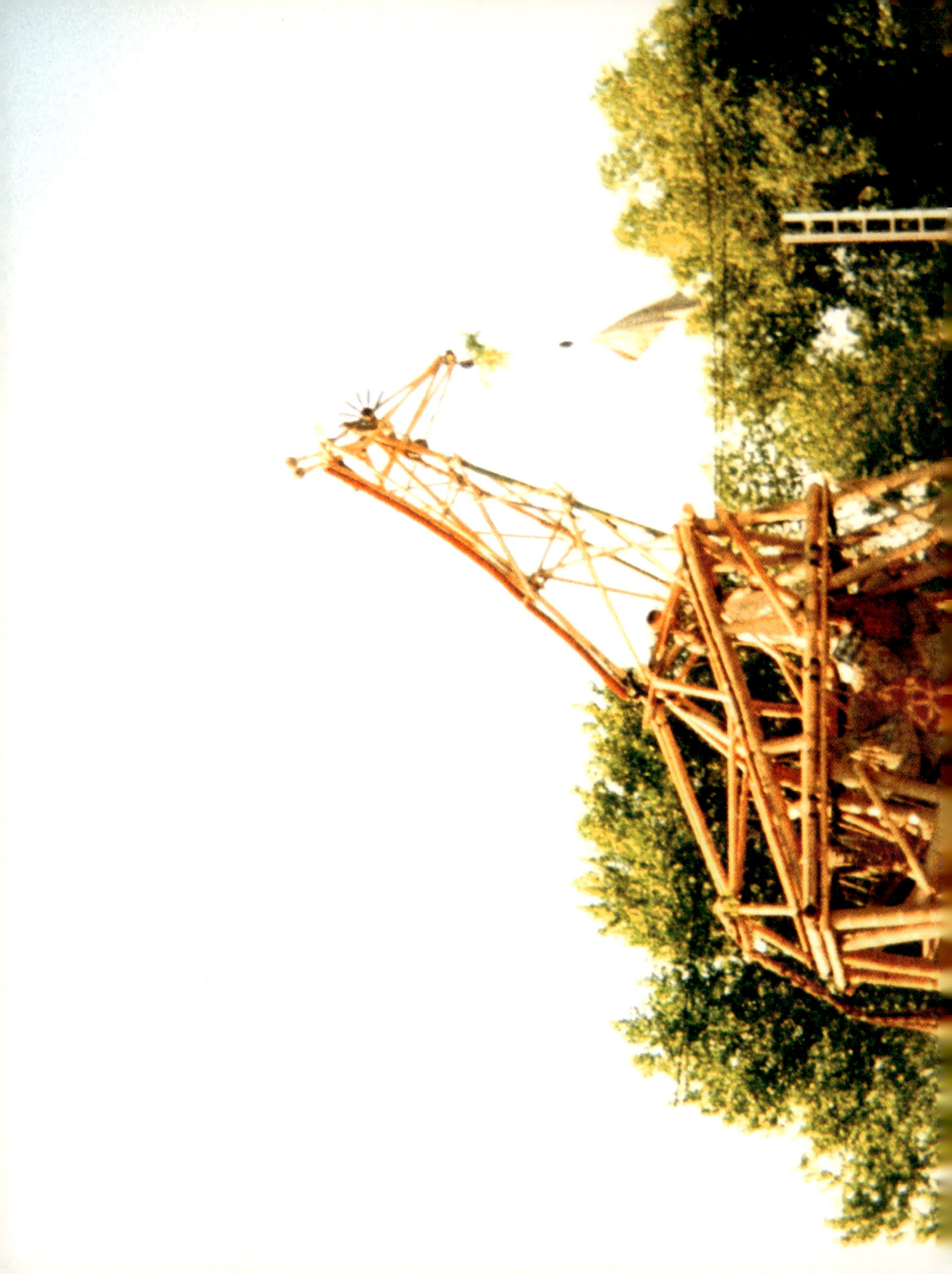

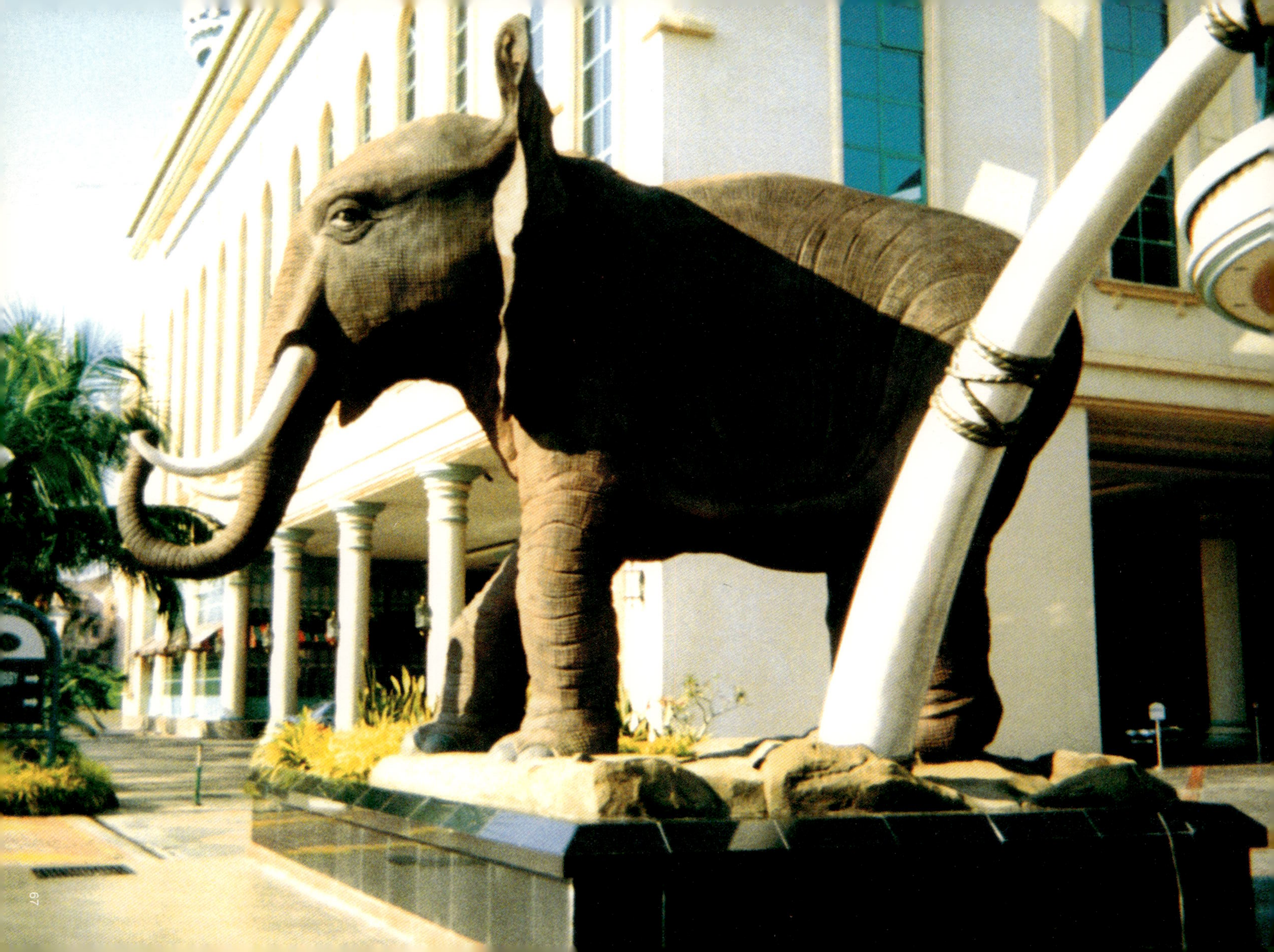

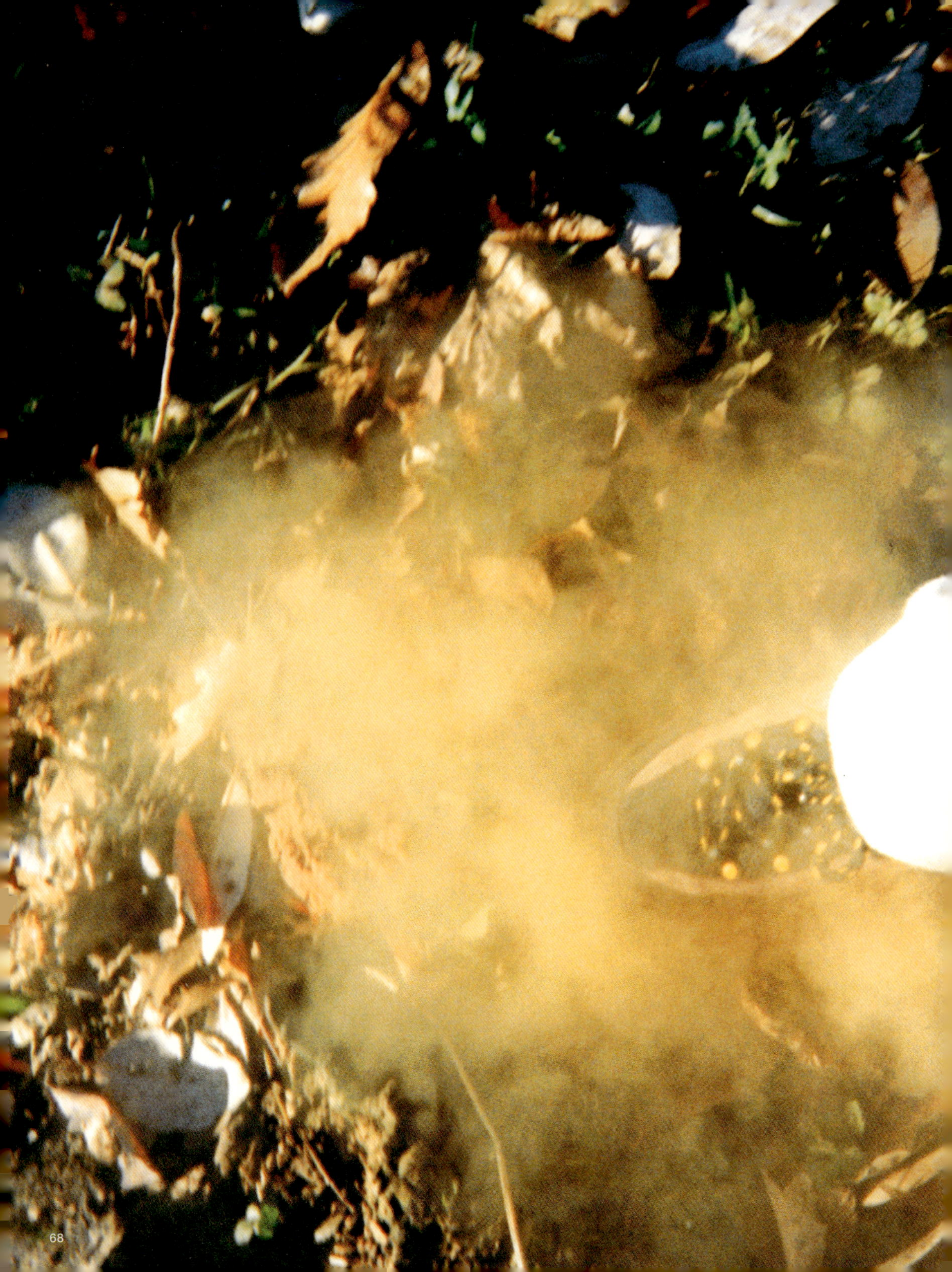

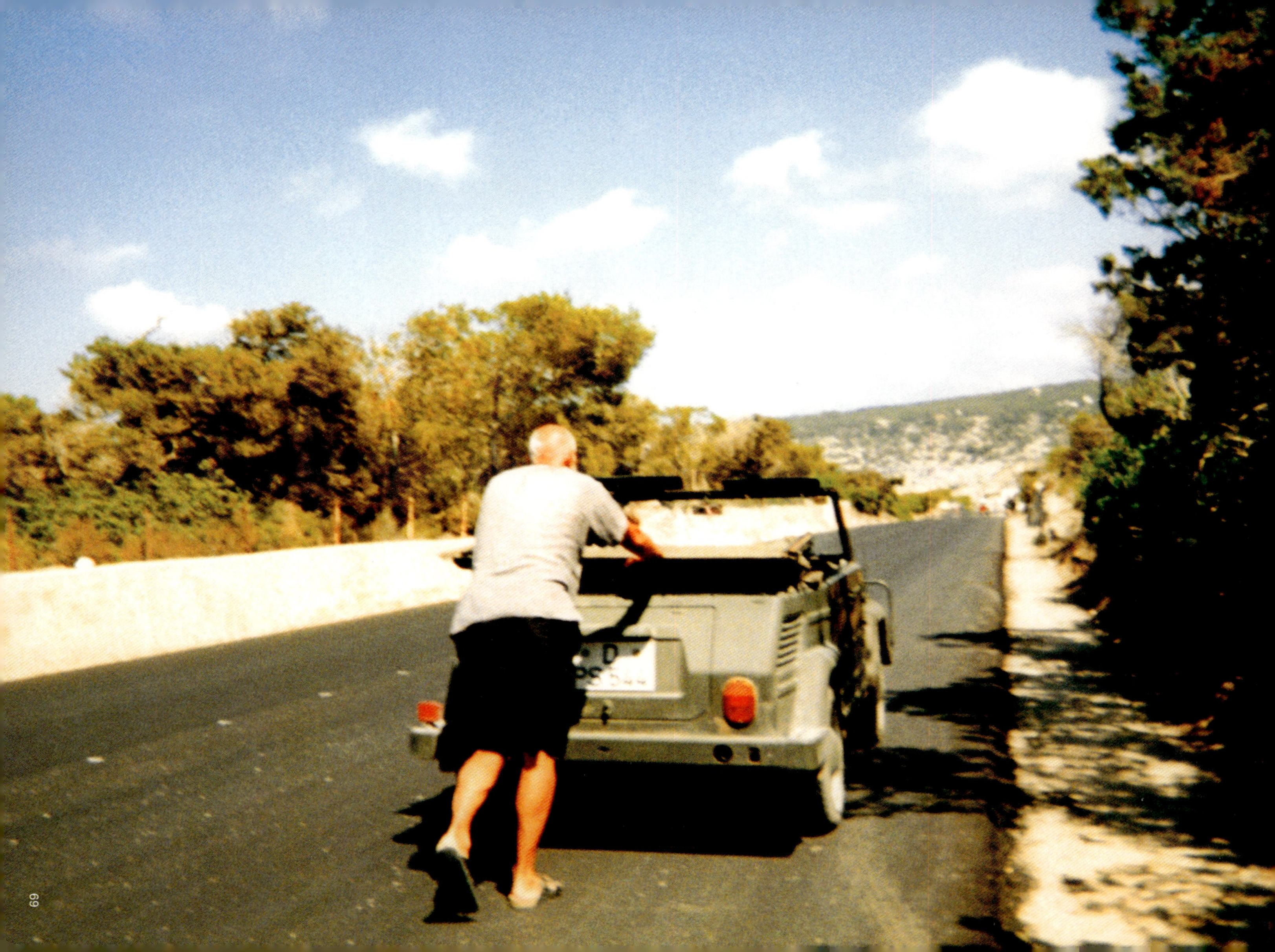

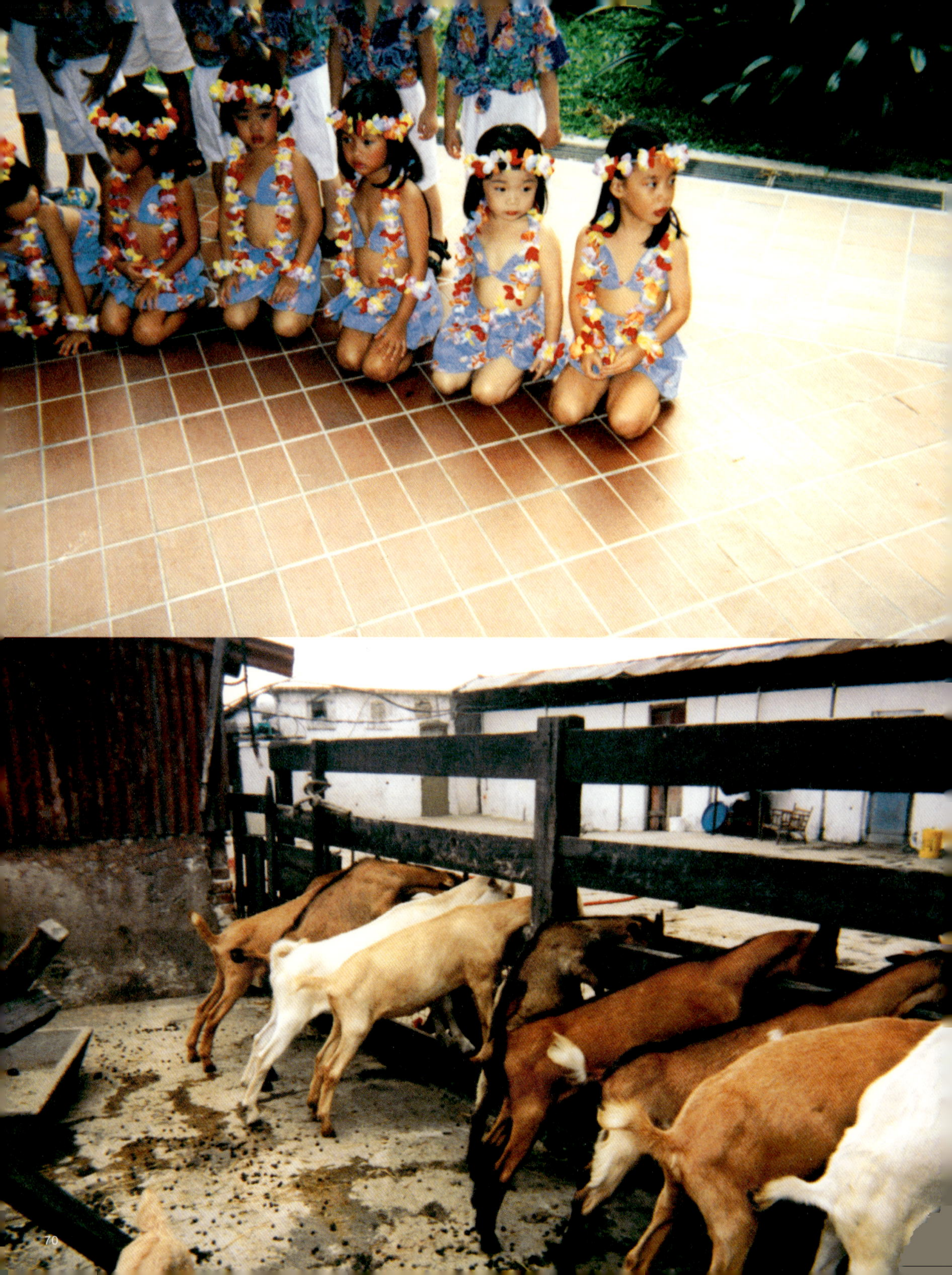

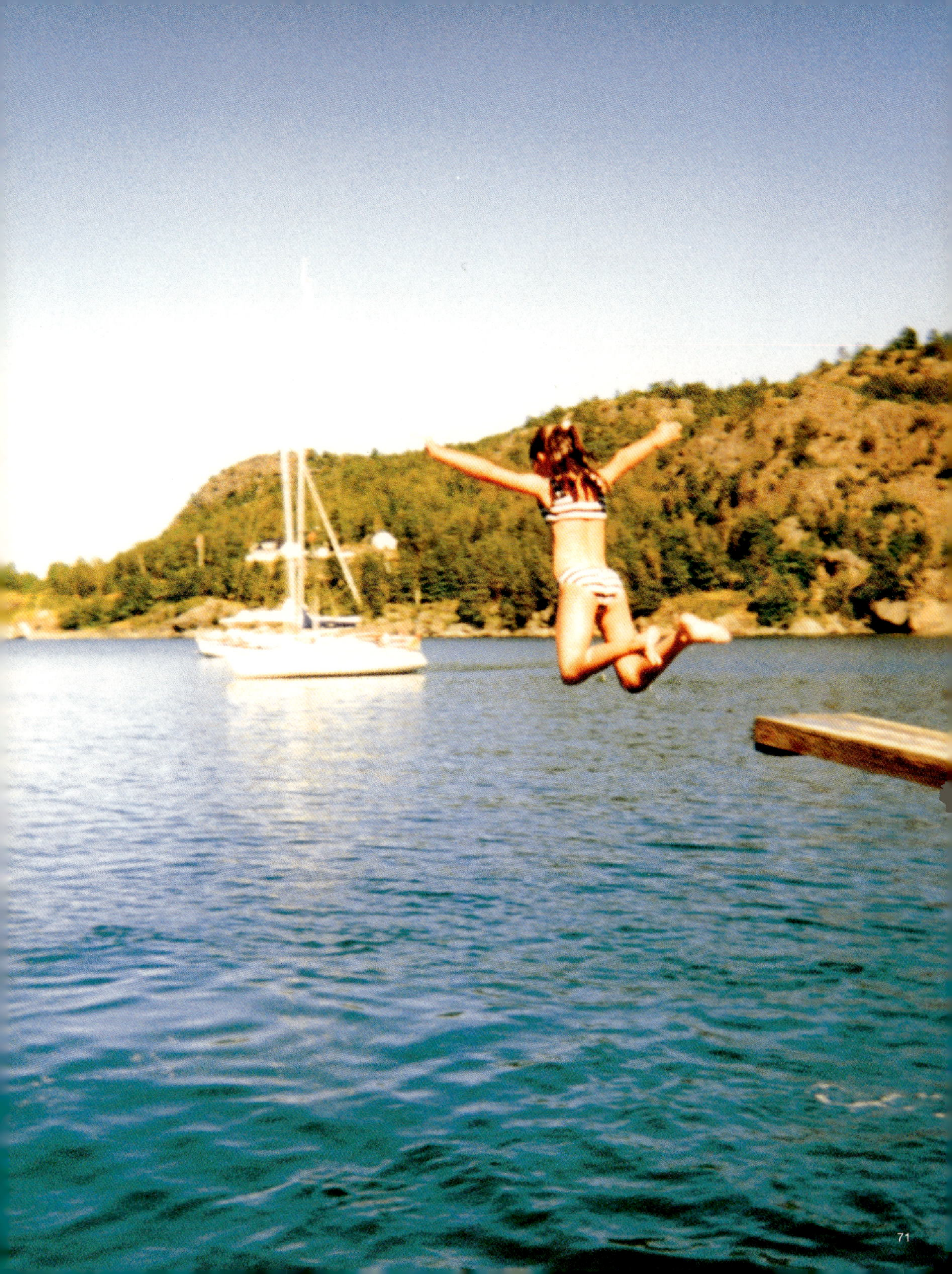

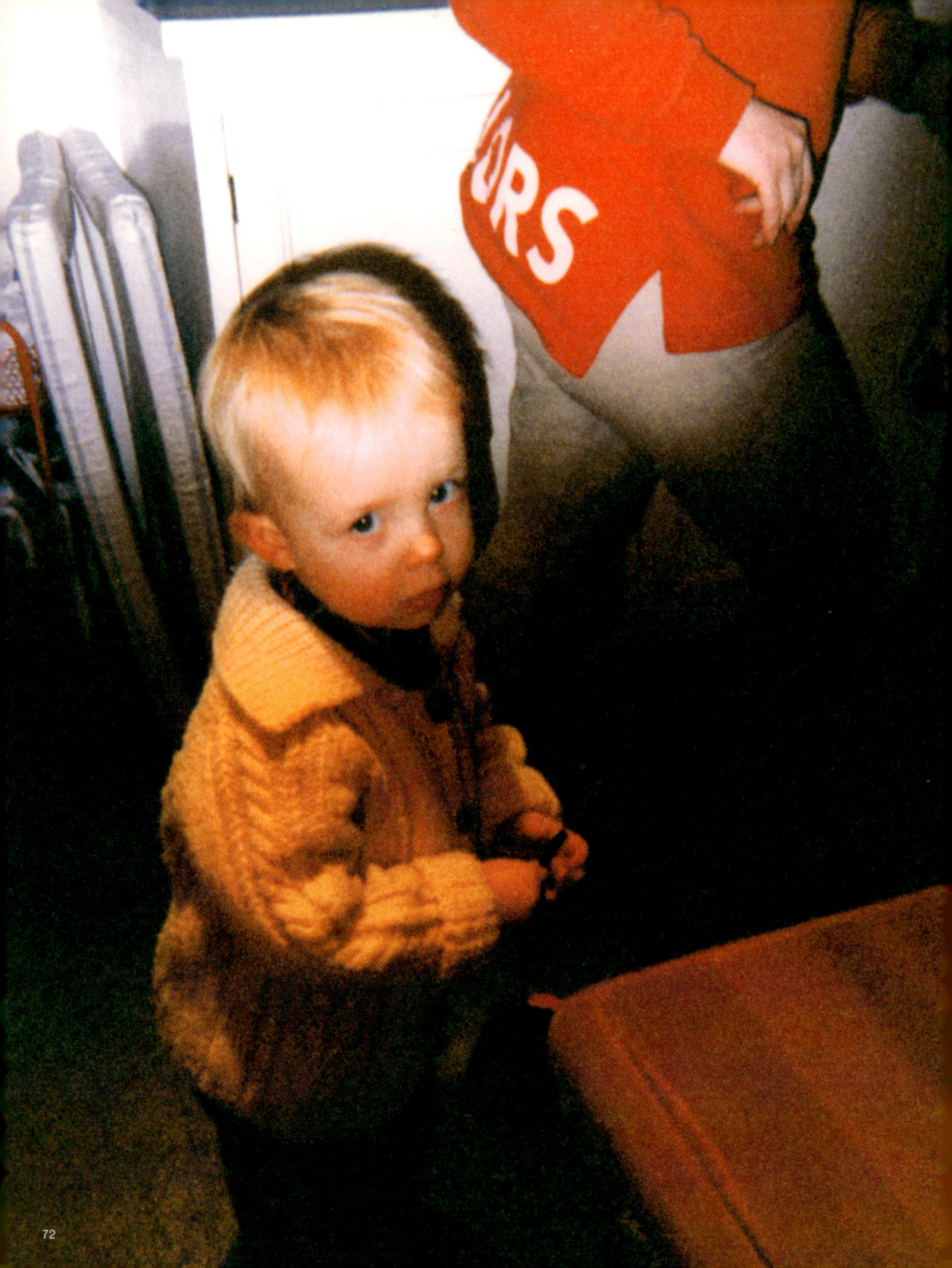
URS

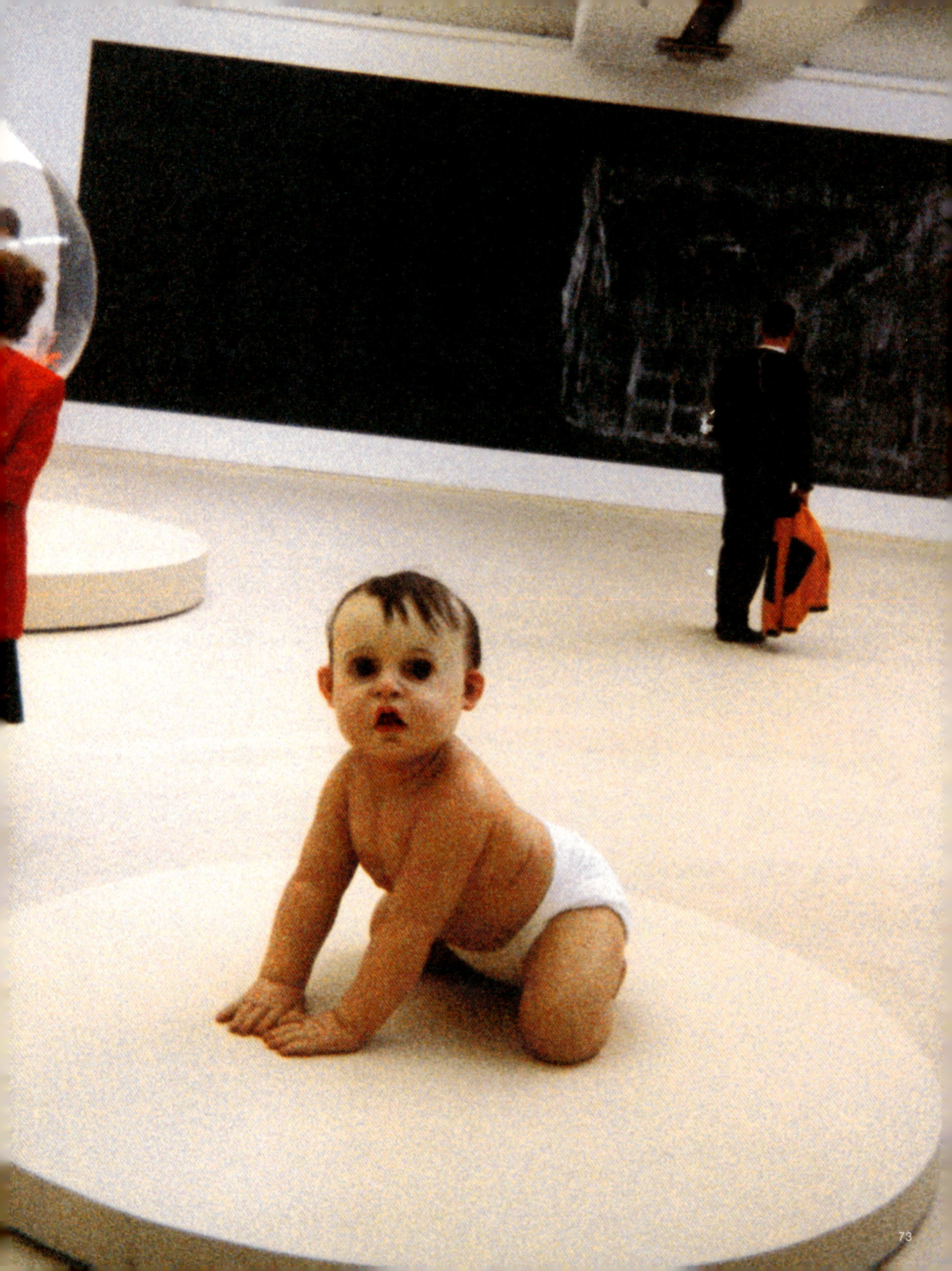

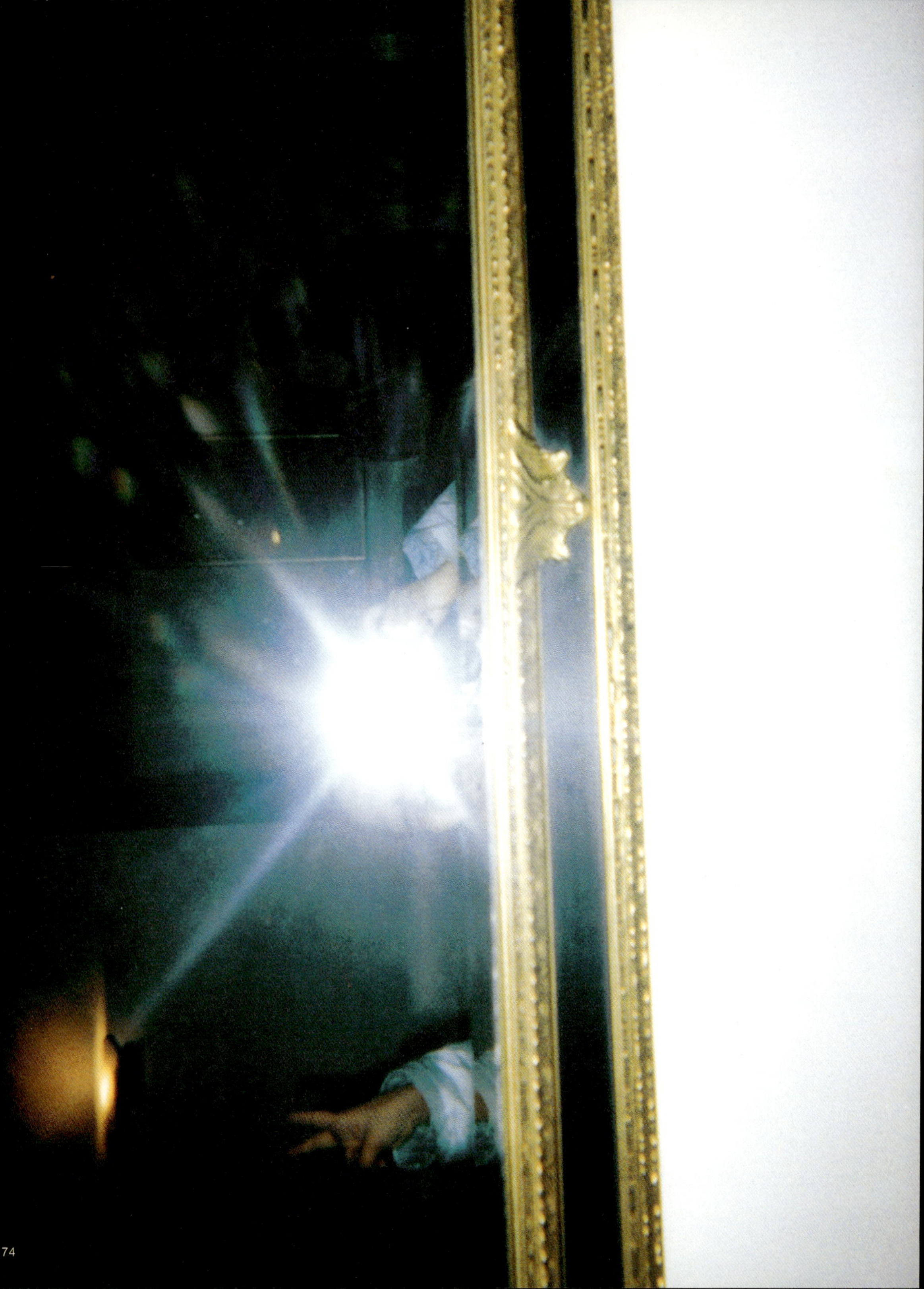

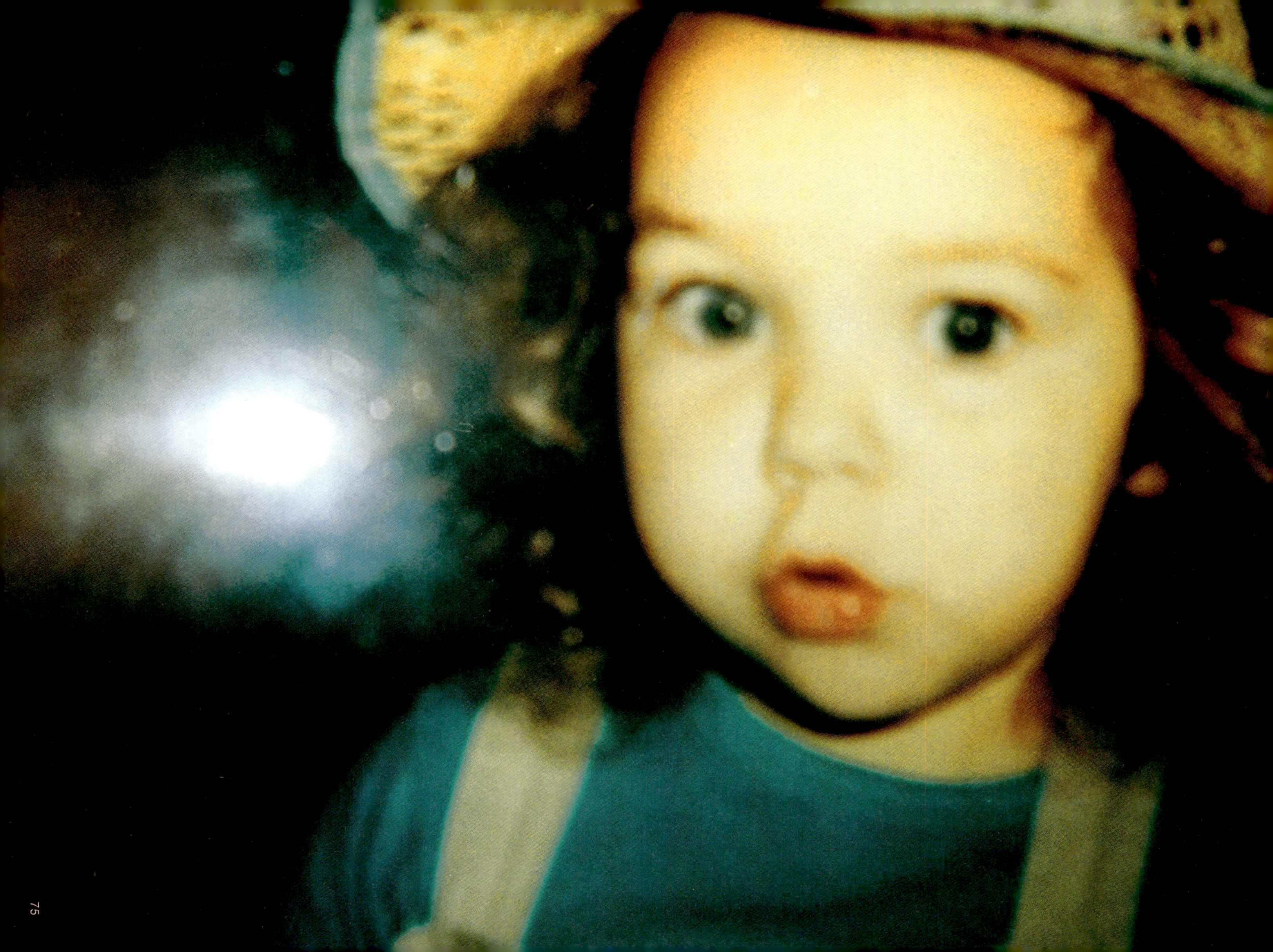

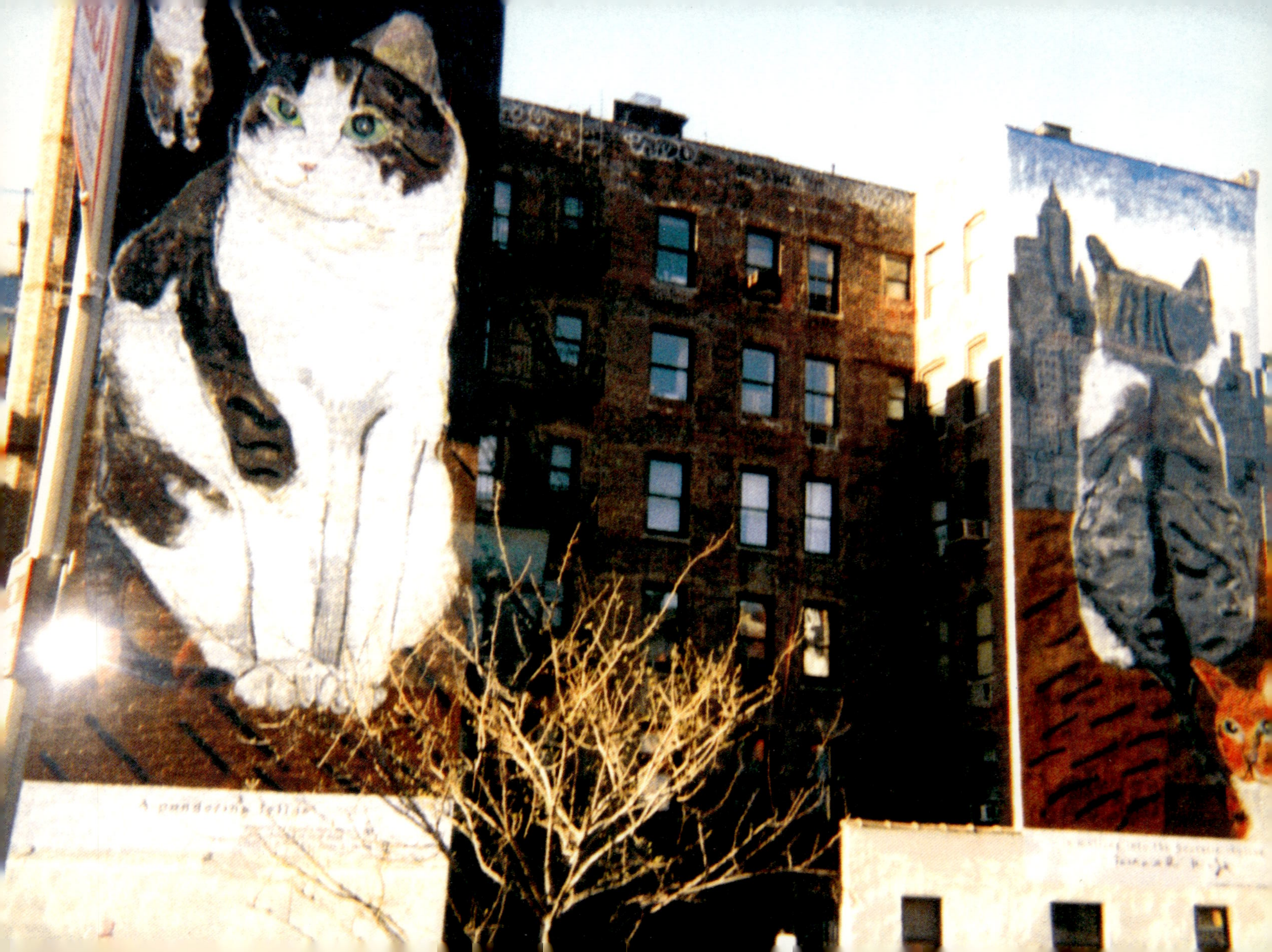
A pondering feline

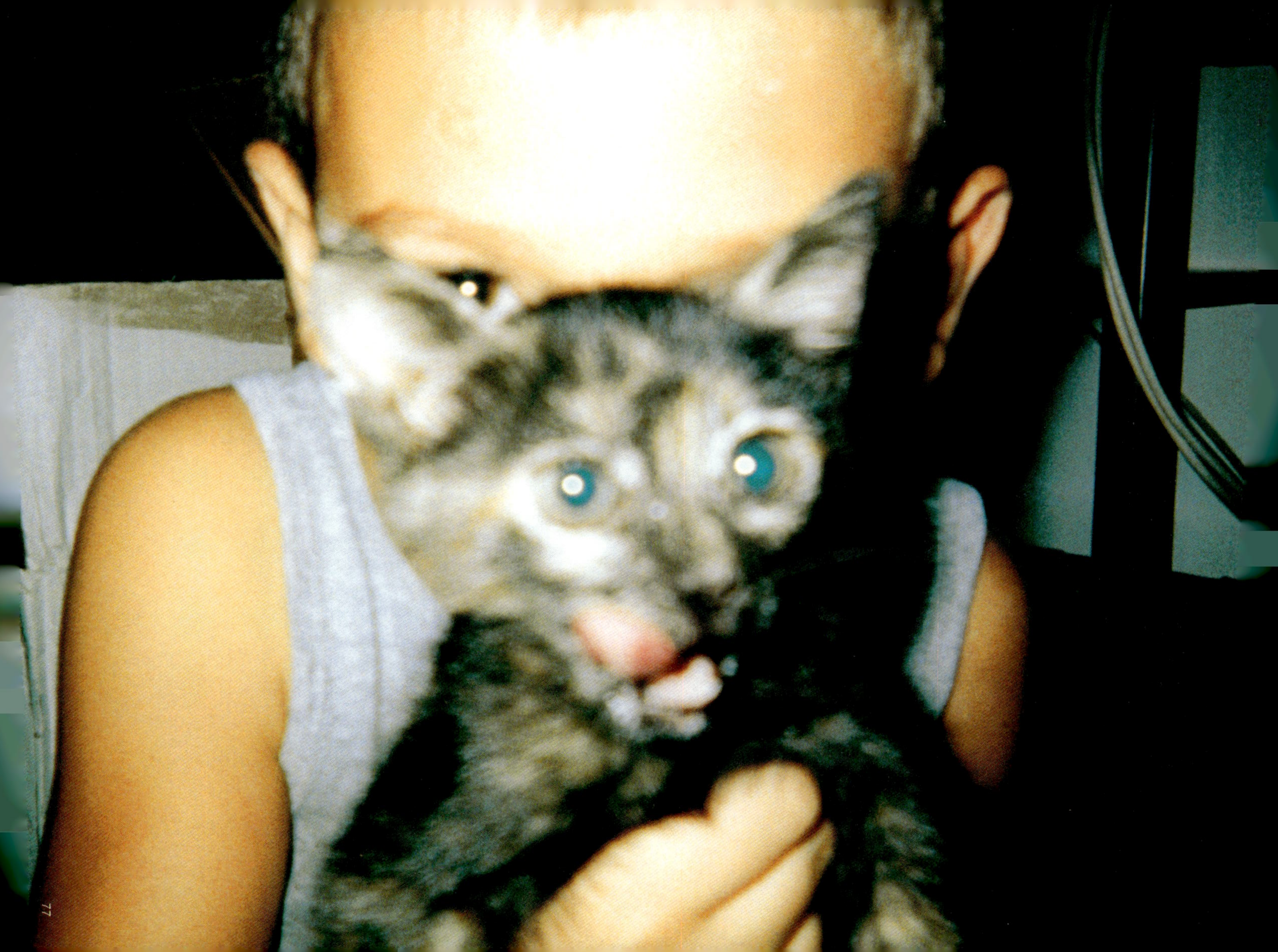

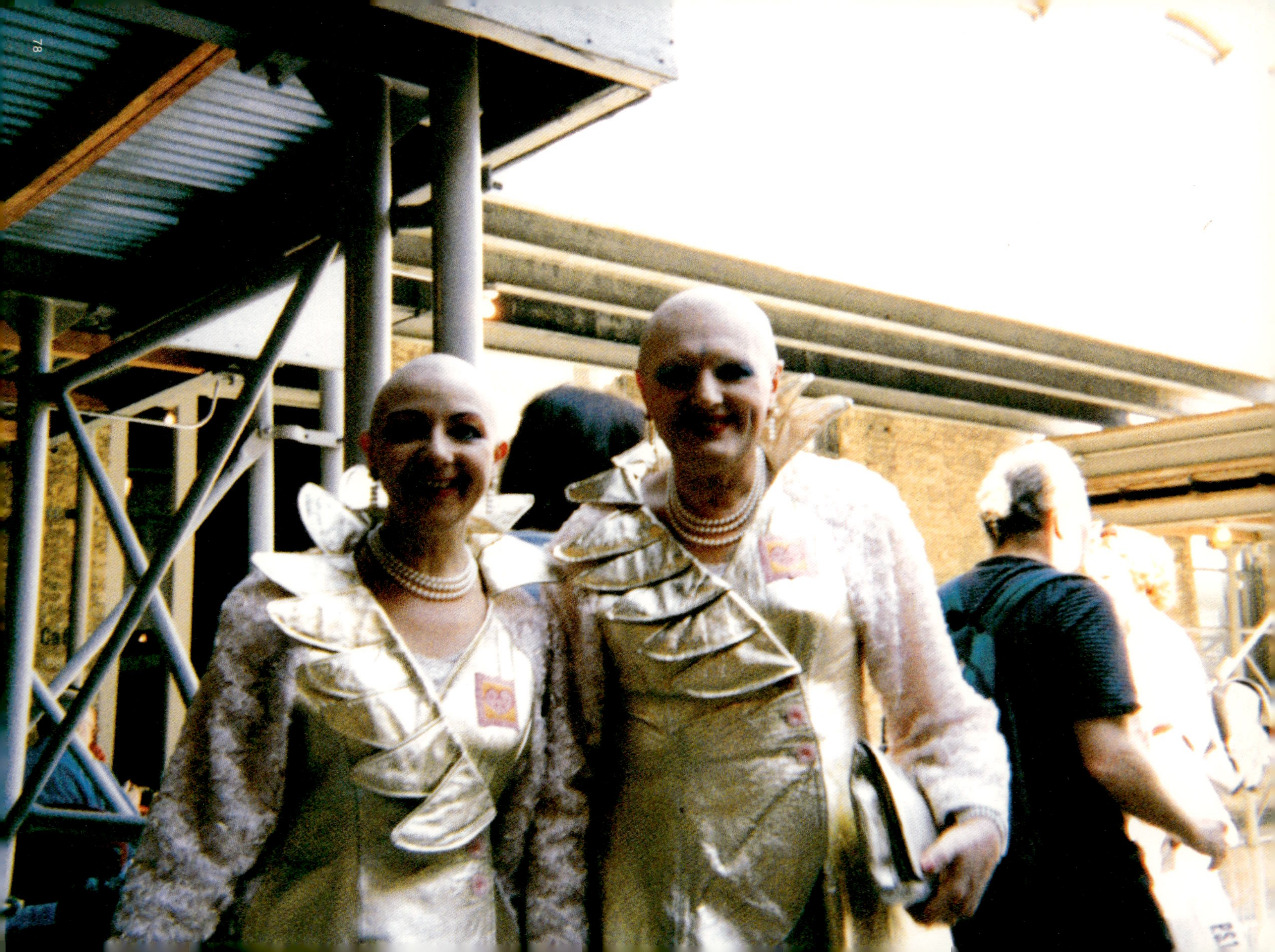

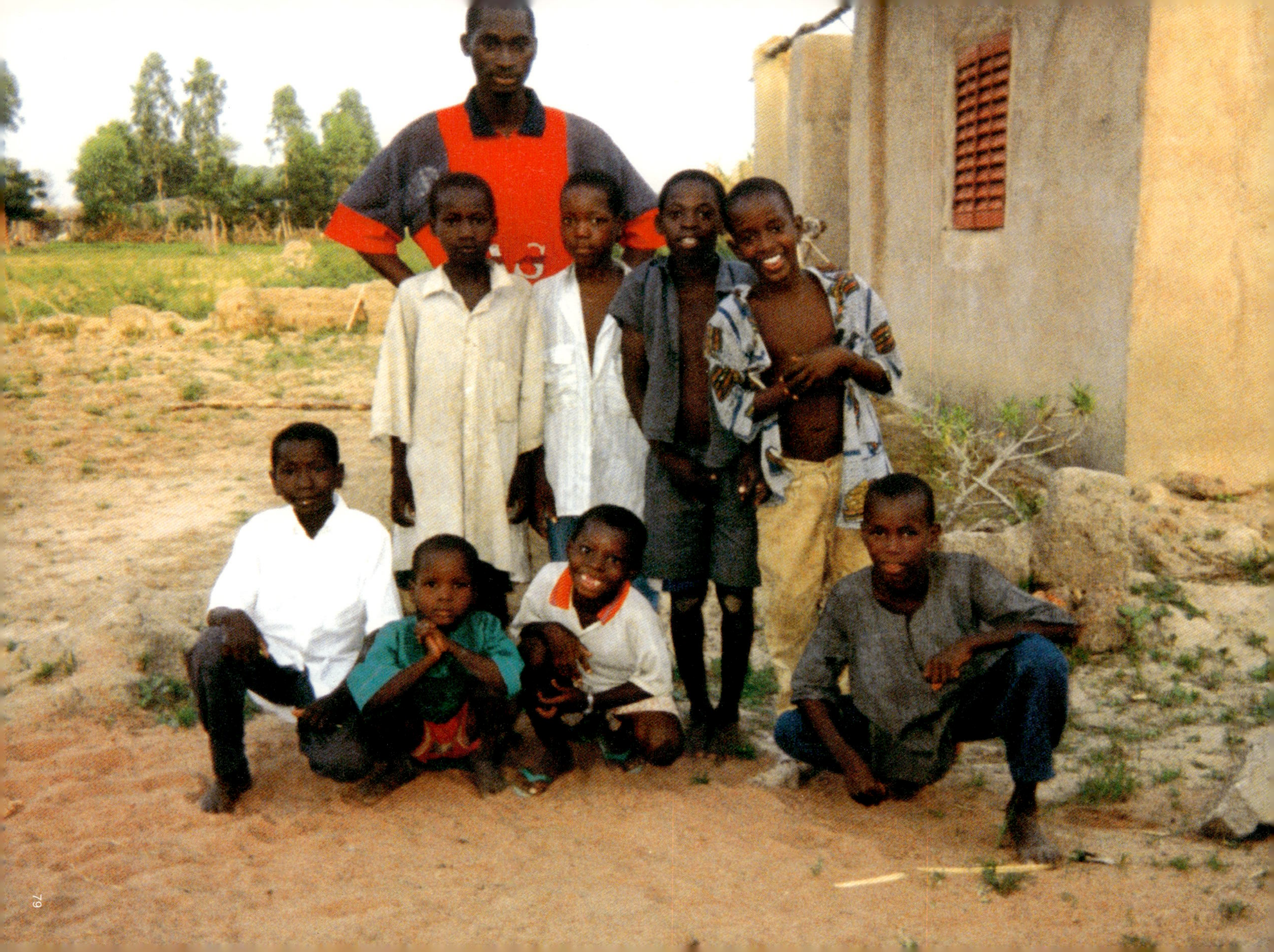

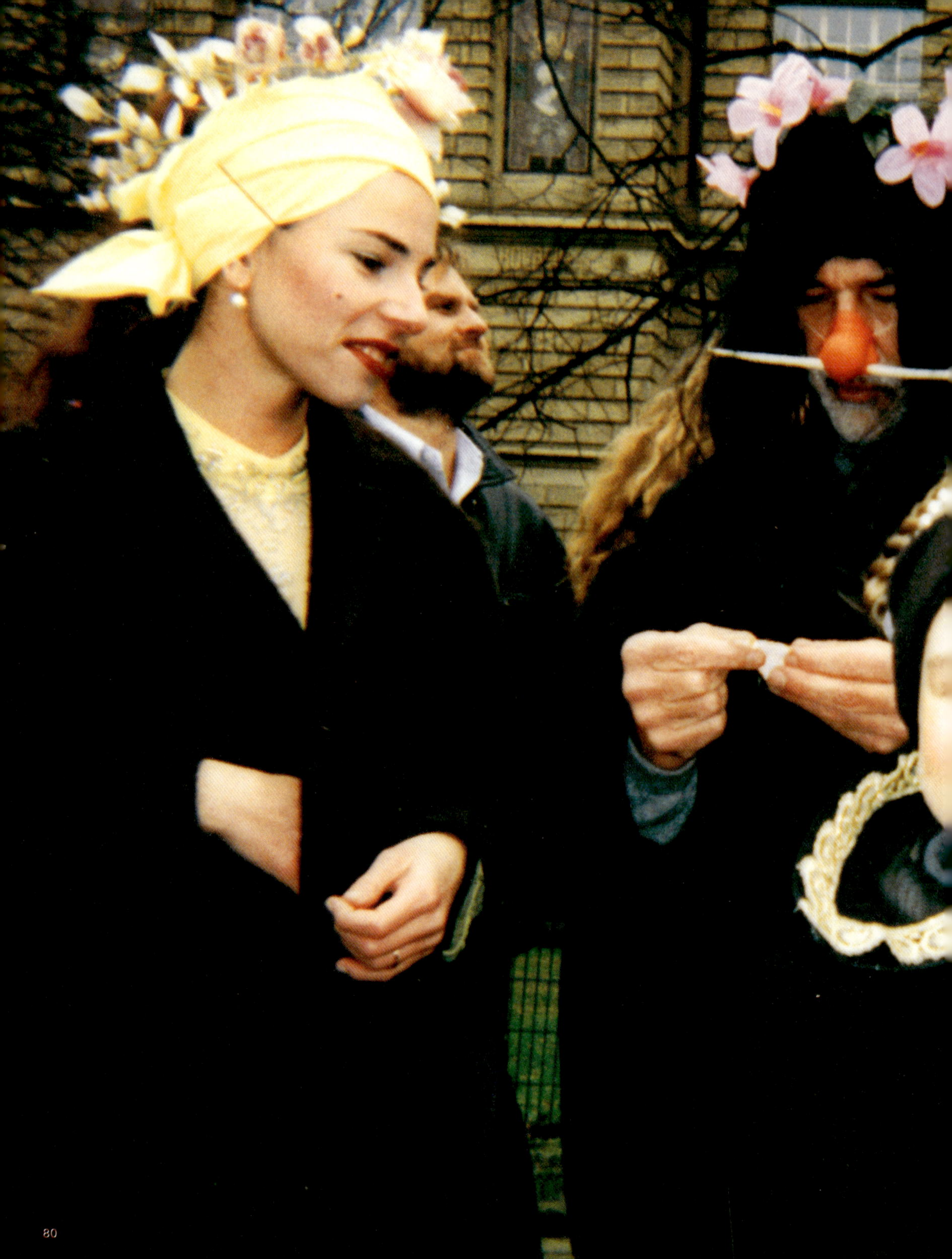

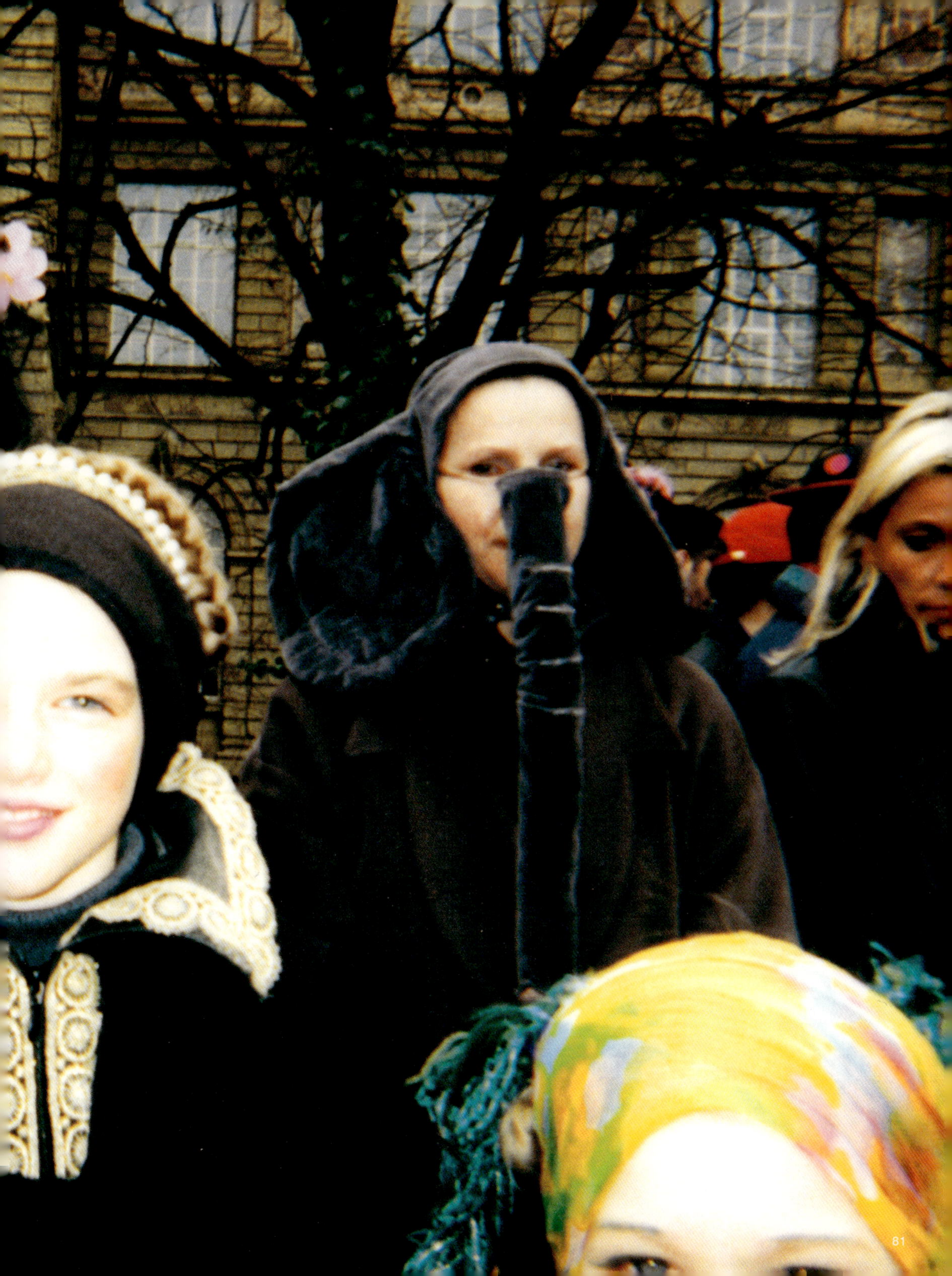

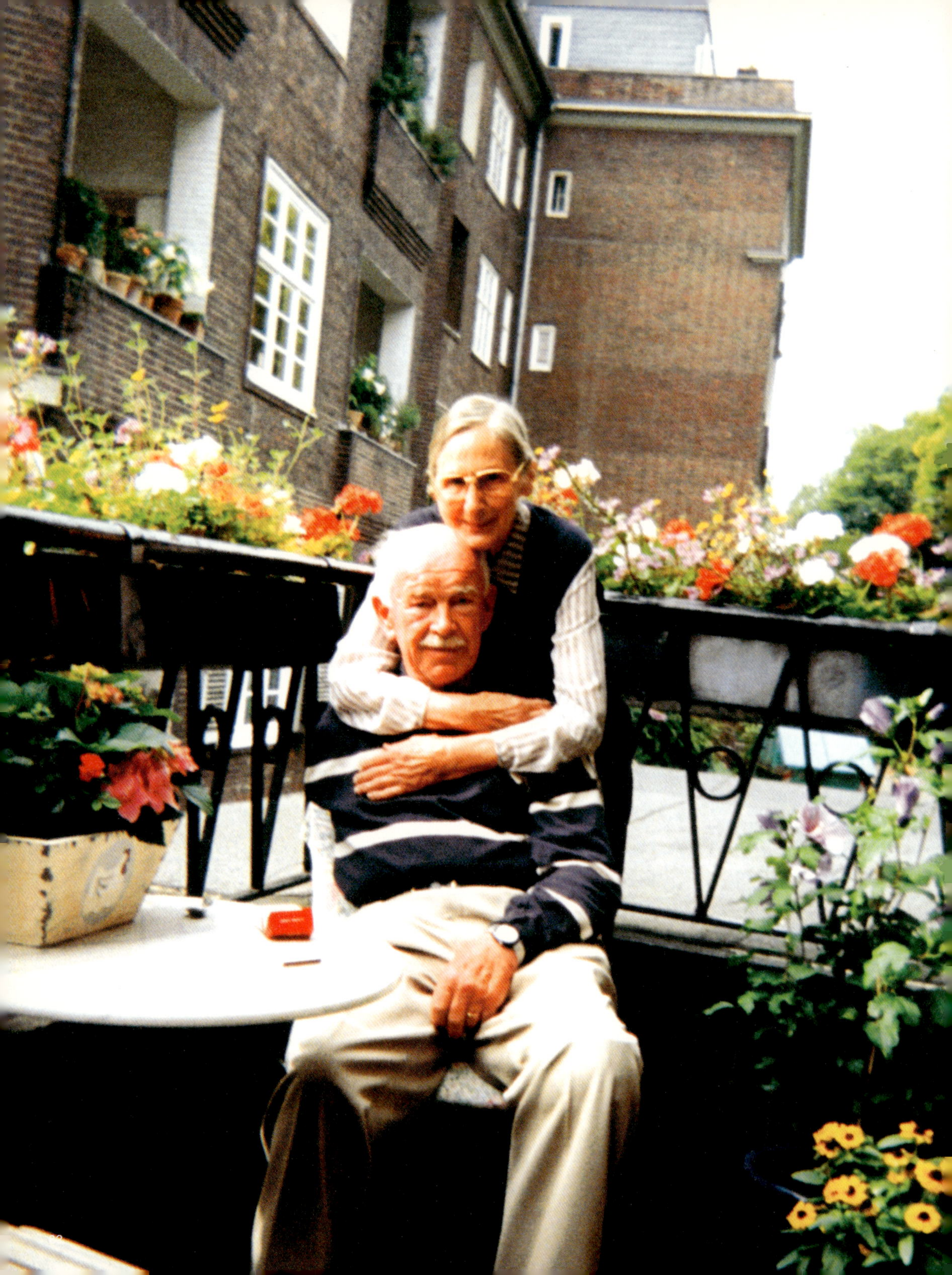

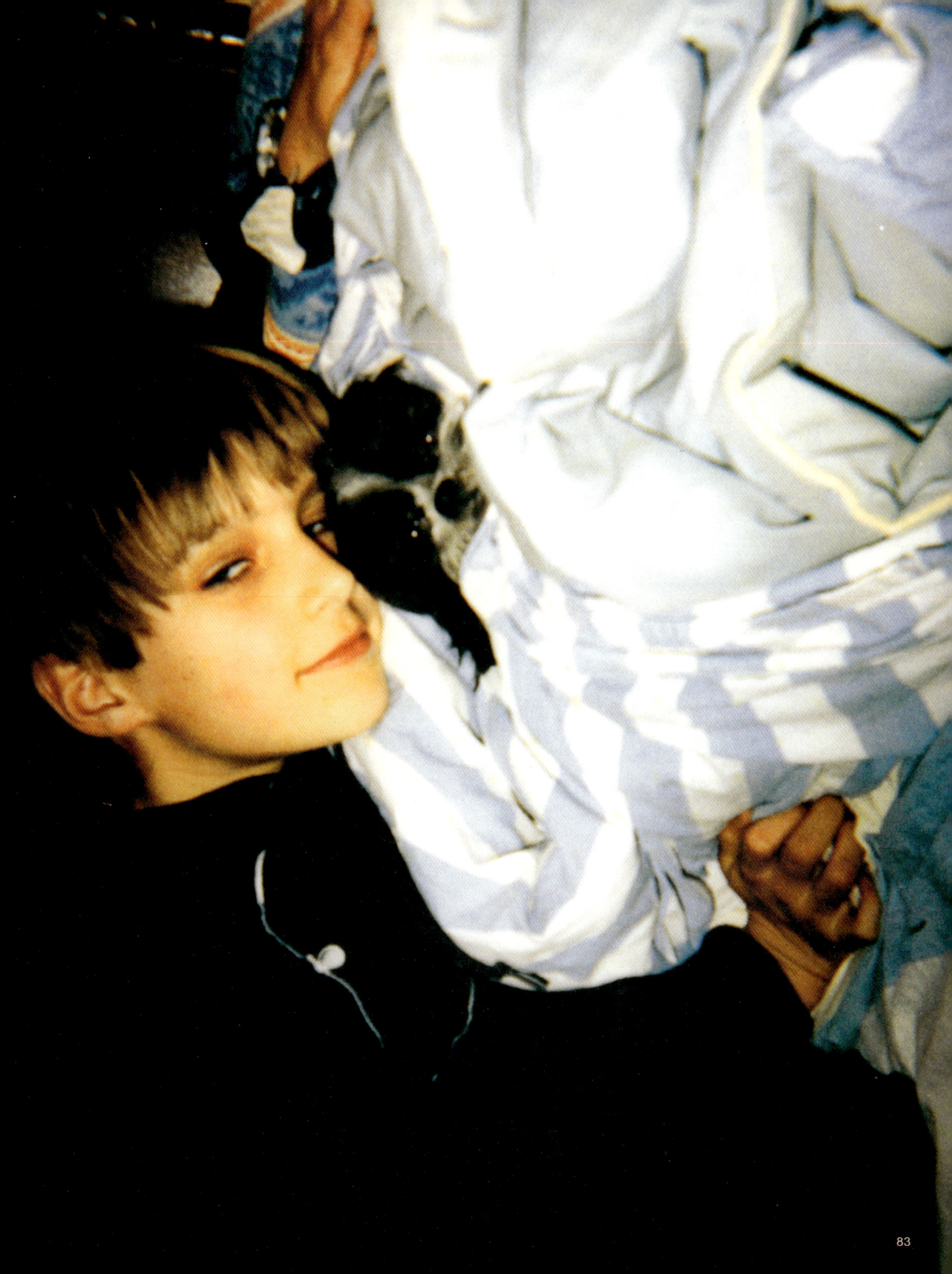

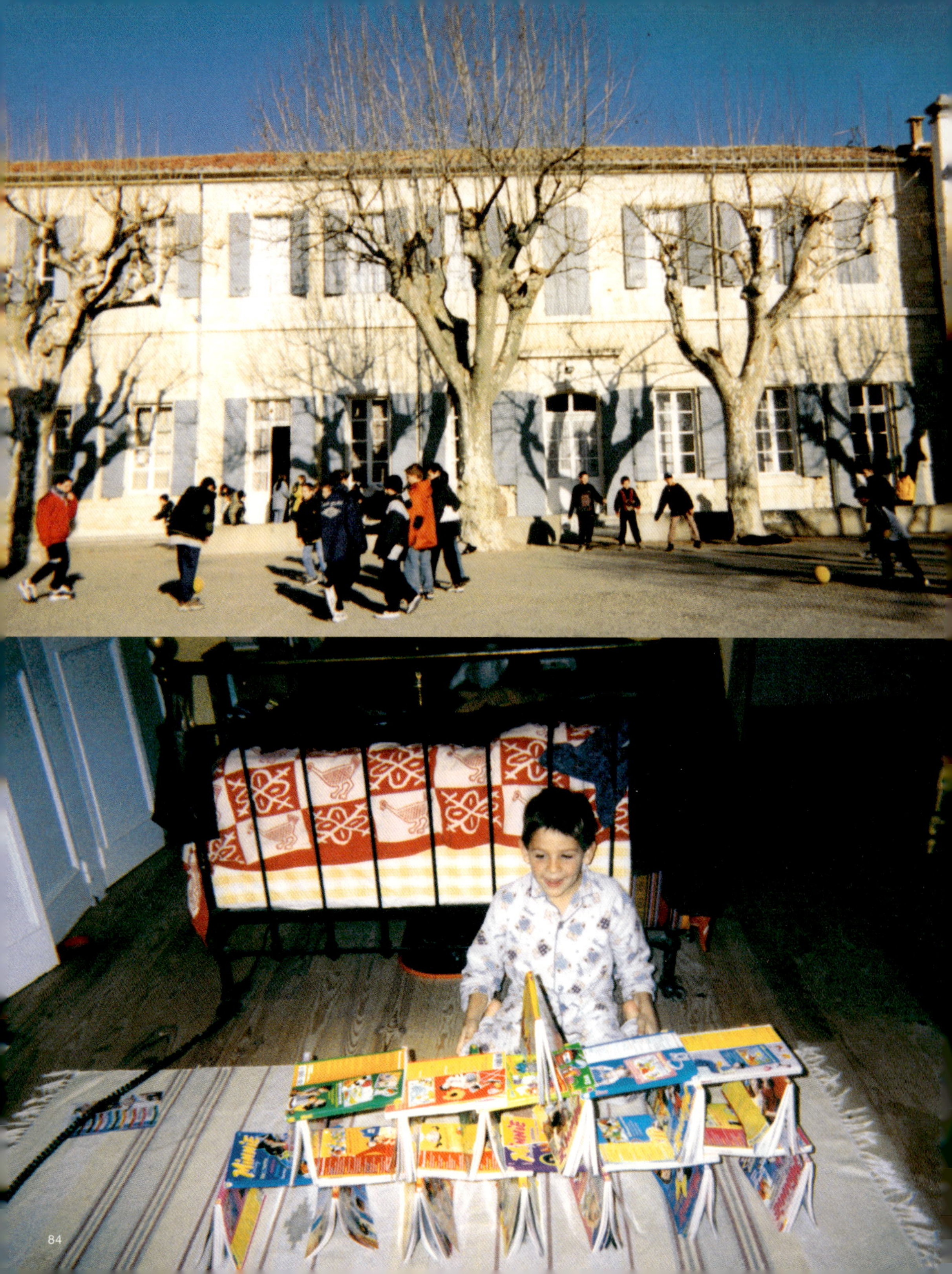

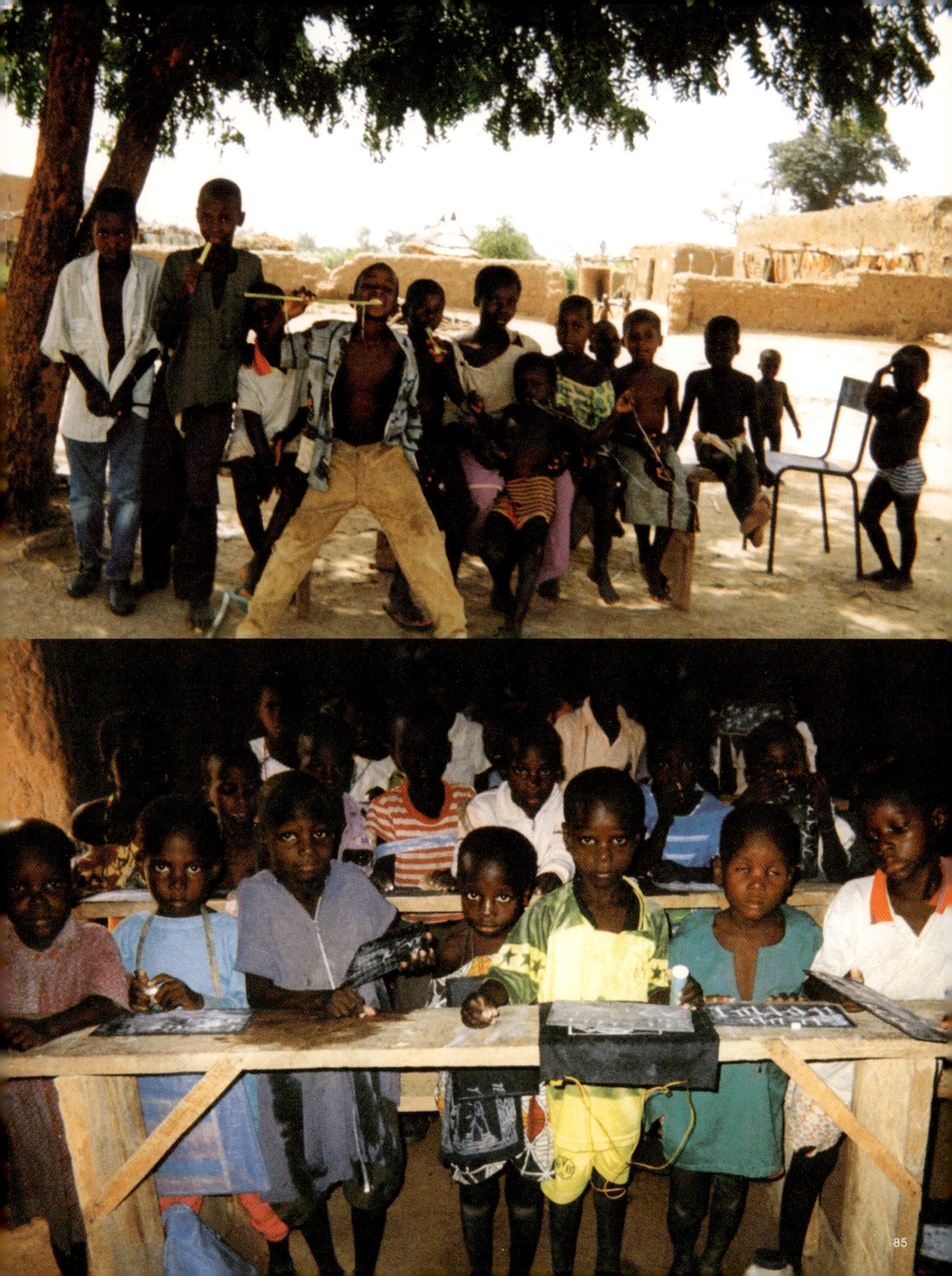

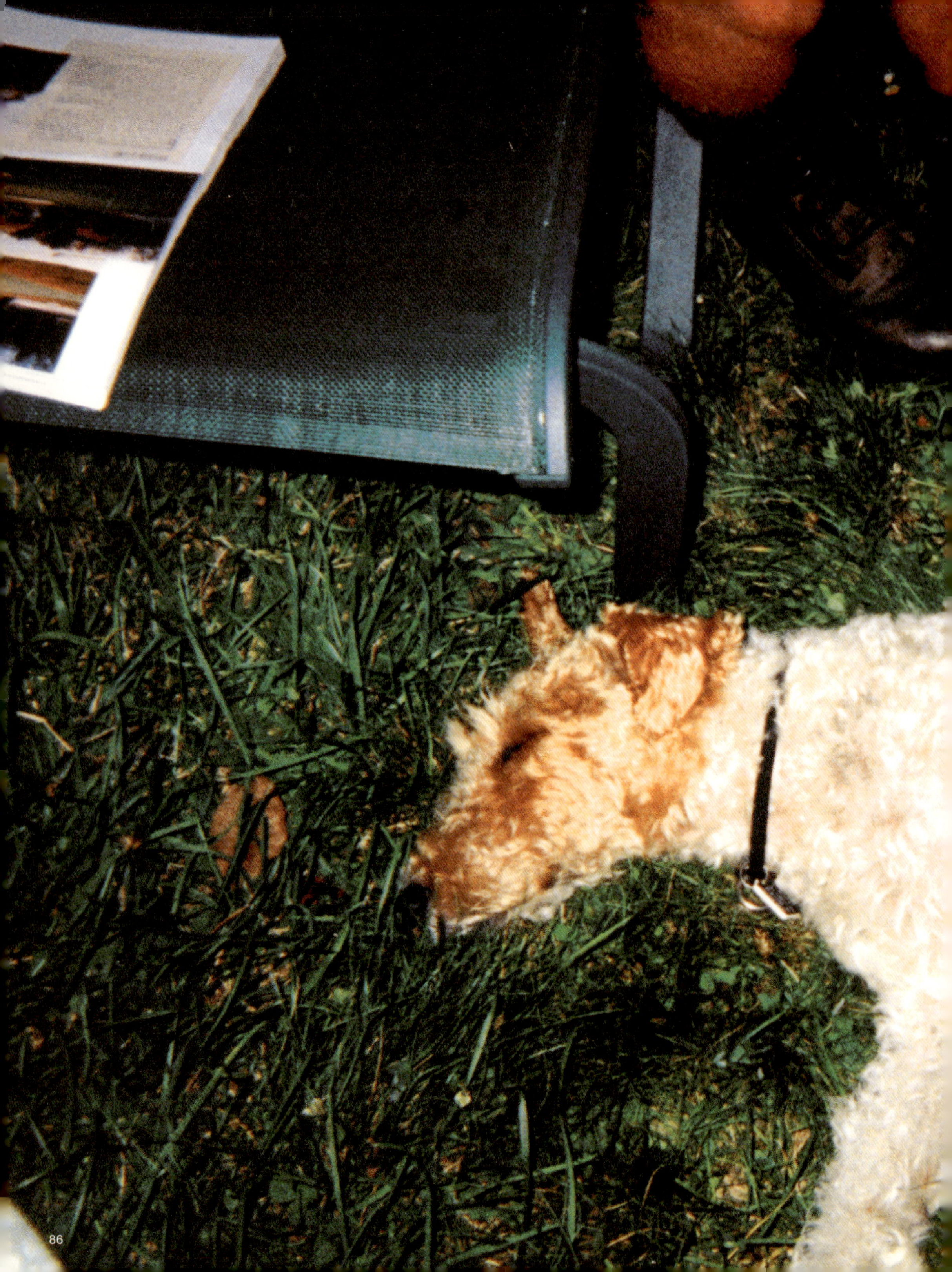

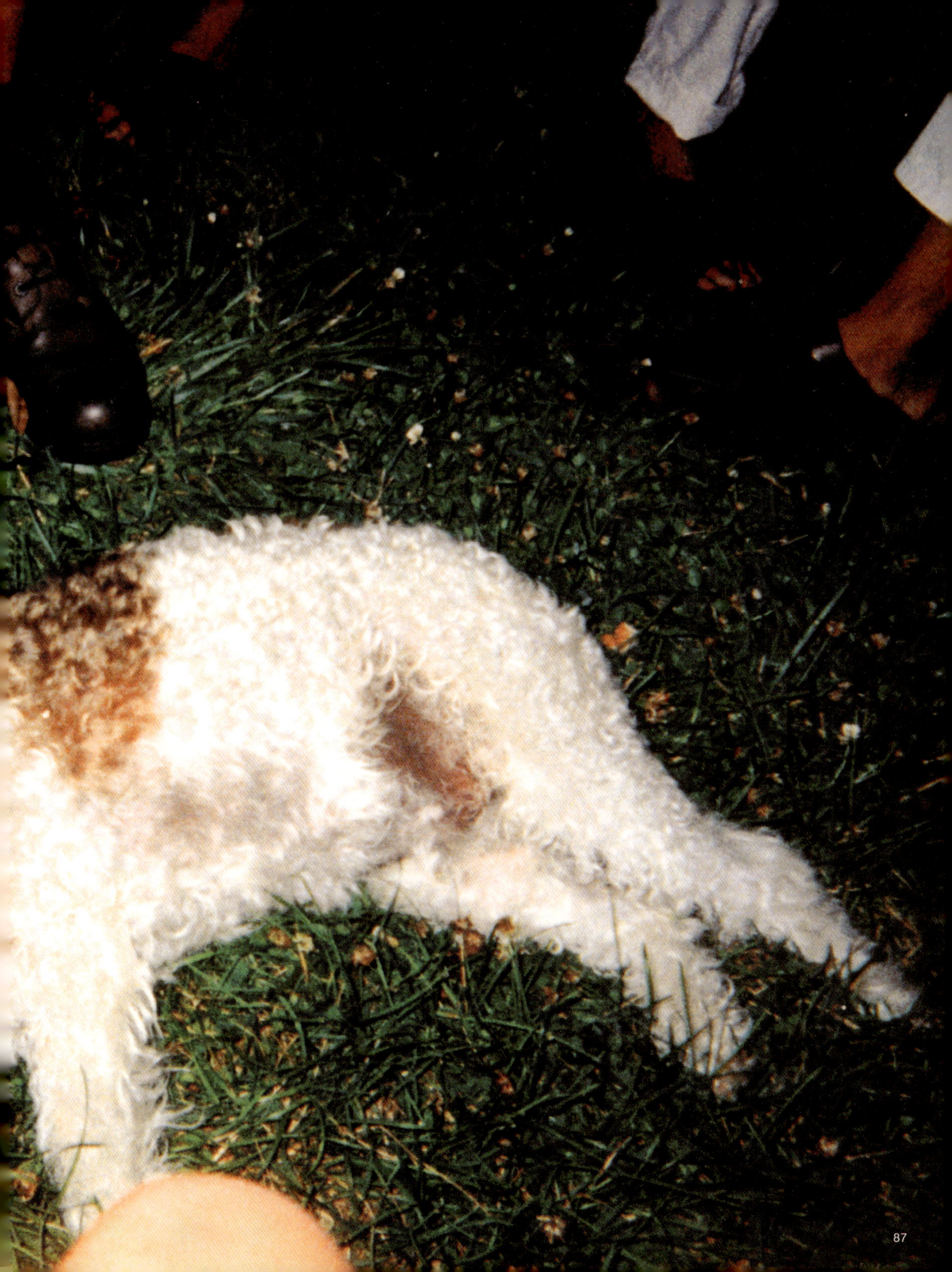

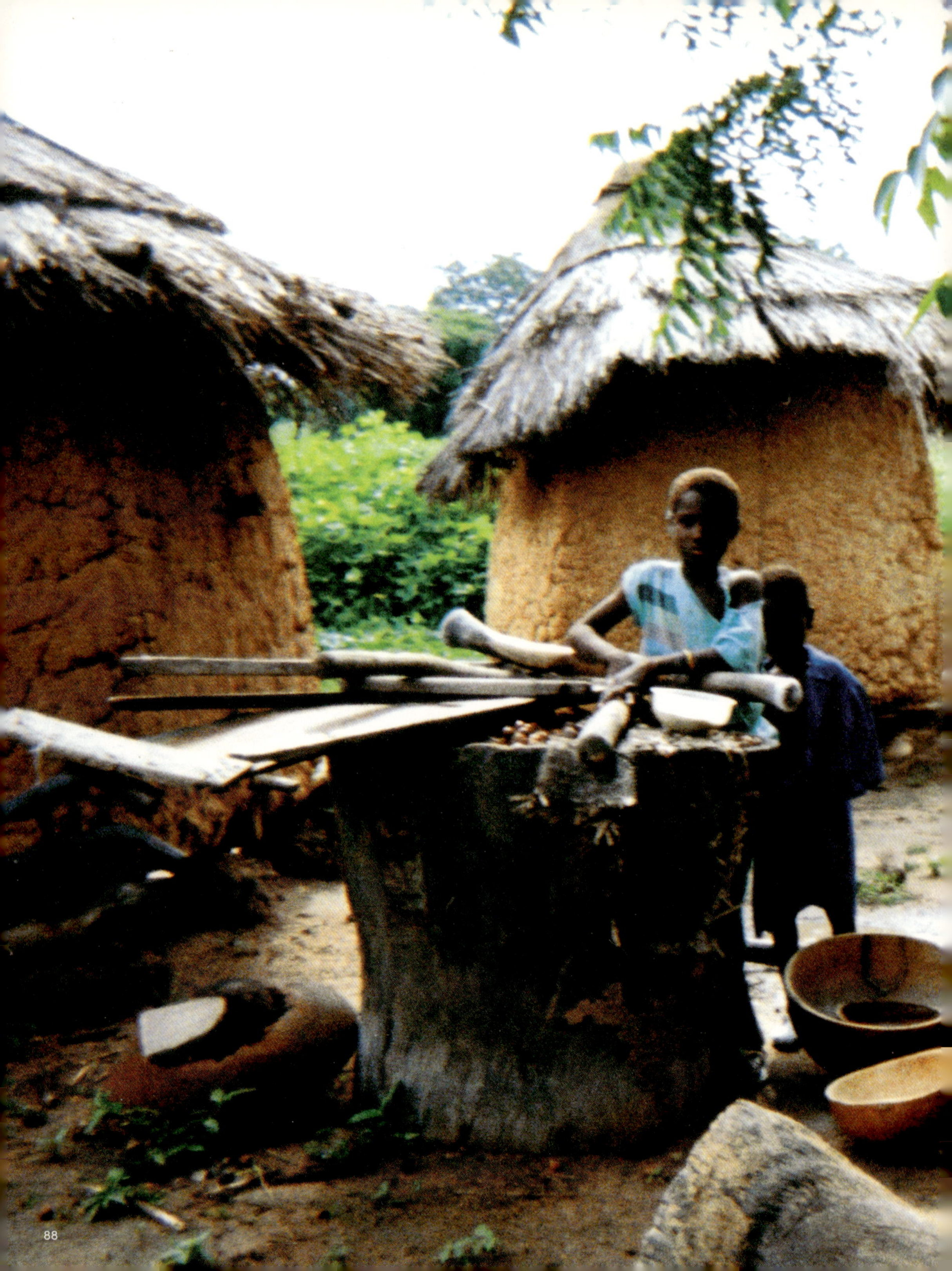

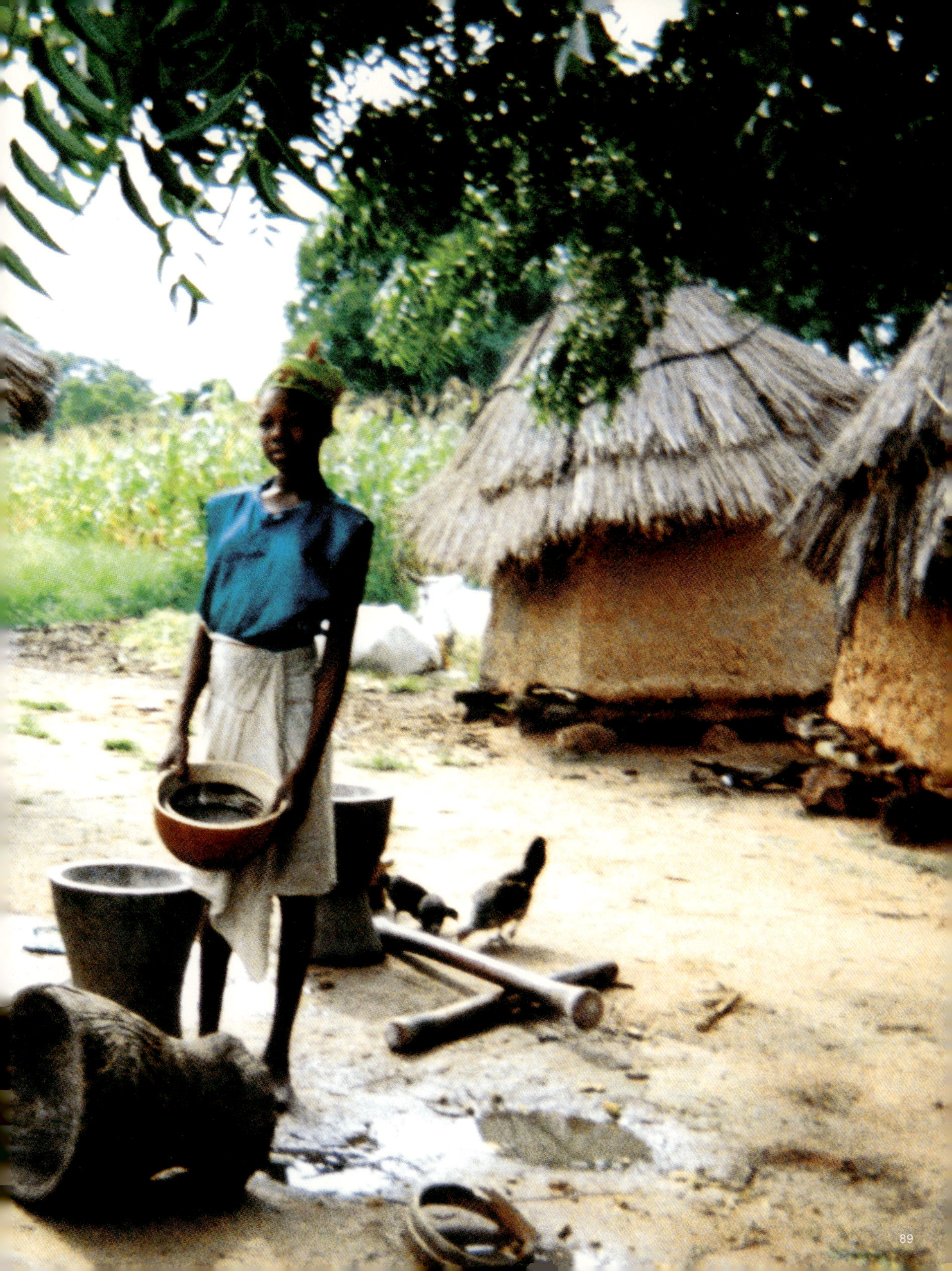

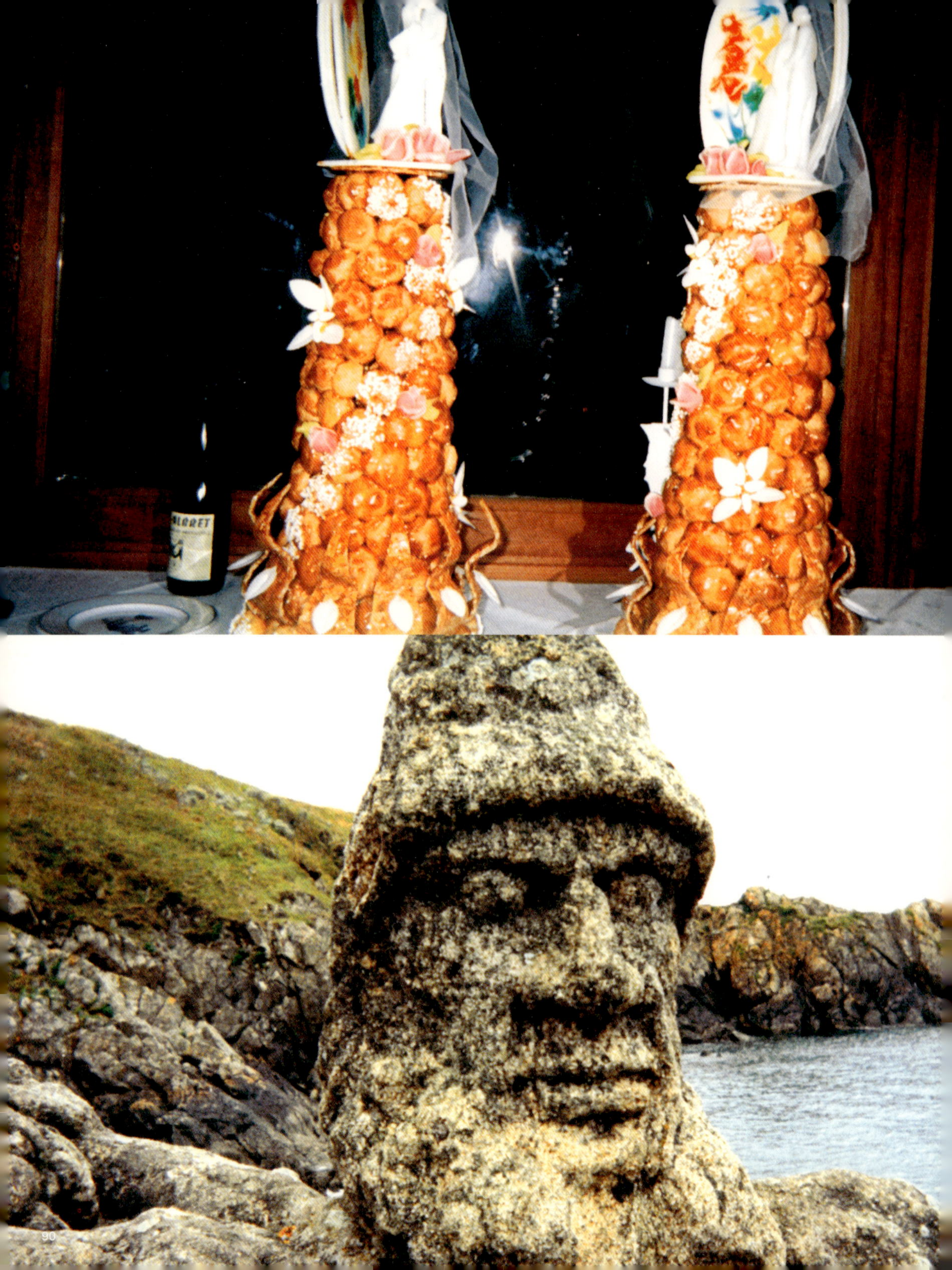

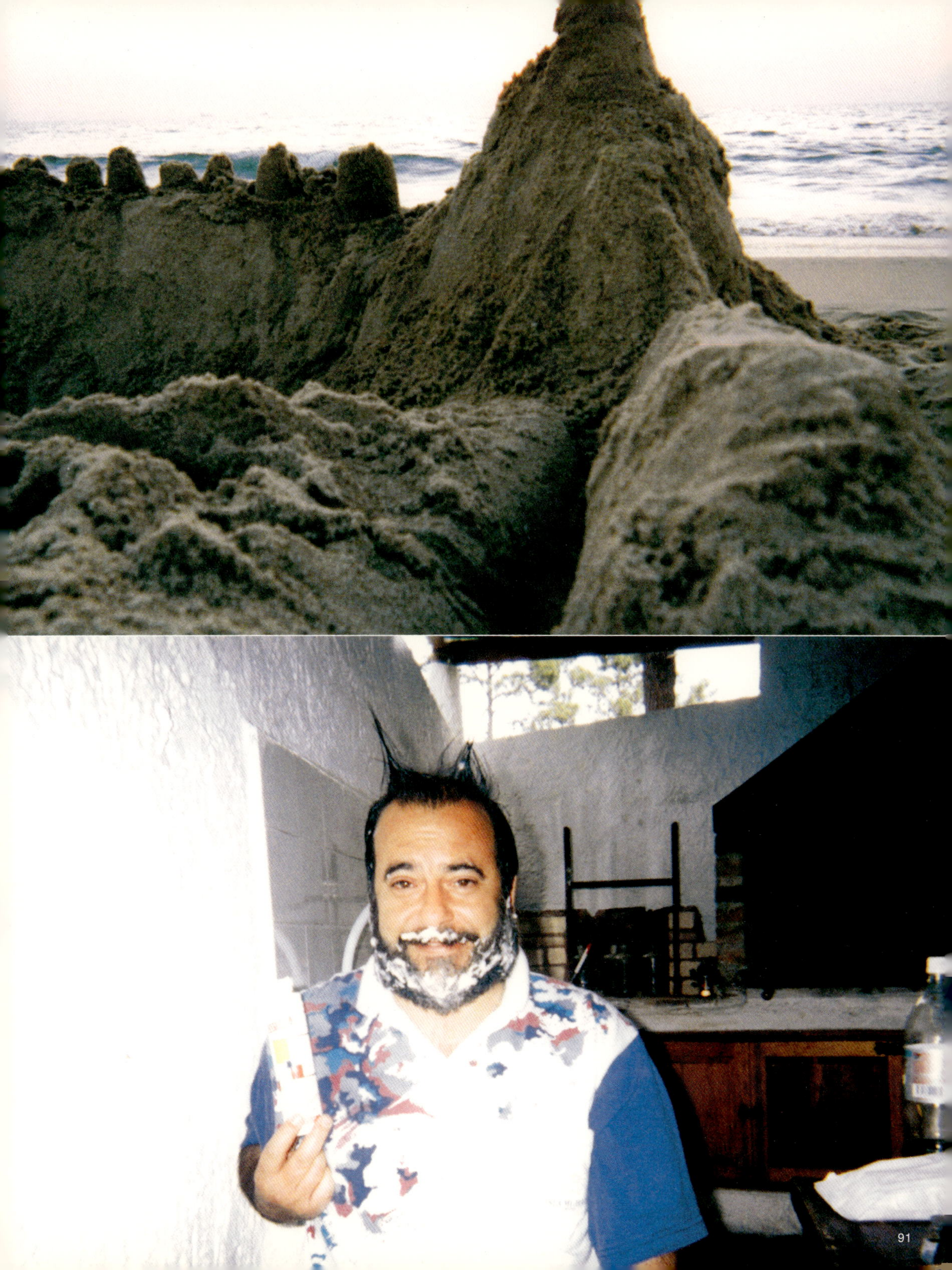

twinkland is published by IPSO FACTO PUBLISHERS, 580, Broadway, suite 700, NYC NY 10012 USA www.ipsofactobooks.com

Publisher : Marc PARENT marcparent@ipsofactobooks.com / Editorial : Marc Parent and Sophie Brosseau
Press : Susanne RICARD-KÖNIG sricard@ipsofactobooks.com
Art Direction : Mathieu TRAUTMANN / Production and Printing : Gerhard STEIDL, Göttingen

Published in the United States by Ipso Facto Publishers Corp.

ISBN : 1-893 263-15-0

Distribution in the United States by :
RIZZOLI INTERNATIONAL PUBLICATIONS
c/o VHPS
175 Fifth Avenue USA-New York, NY 10010
Phone : ++(1) 800 488 5233 Fax : ++(1) 800 258 2769

Printed and bound in Germany.

Visit our website for more: www.ipsofactobooks.com

Special warm thanks & congratulations from the Publisher to all the children-photographers as well as to Sophie Brosseau, Emma Bland & Kathrin Kollmann.

The Publisher would like to extend his special thanks to EASTMAN KODAK for having given Ipso Facto Publishers more than 300 MAX flash cameras, to François-Xavier Deler & PHOTO SERVICE for their contribution to the development & printing of the pictures, as well as to Valérie PINCHEMEL, David HIRON & their team at the Rue du Commerce PHOTO SERVICE photo lab in the 15th arrondissement of Paris.

CHILDREN-PHOTOGRAPHERS :	PAGES:
Catalina BRISKI - Argentina	23 - 29 - 43 - 48 - 91(down)
Ornella CATTANEO - Uruguay	11 - 16 - 17 - 18 - 22 - 42 - 44 - 65 (down) - 70 (down) - 75
Brendan DUNNE - Italy	8 - 9 - 13 - 19 - 20 - 23 - 52 (up)
Charlotte de GIVRY - Provence	10 - 50 - 66 - 84
Jennifer FLORES - USA	28 - 49 - 54
Anja FOUGEA - France/India	Back cover - 32 - 44 - 91 (up)
Nicholas von GUIONNEAU - UK	27 - 39 - 40 - 41 - 52 (down) - 72
Madou KOULIBALY - Mali	30 (up) - 58 (up) - 78 (down) - 85
Sada KOULIBALY - Mali	53 (up) - 55 - 56
Vibeke MAGNUS - Norway	Front cover - 4 - 6 - 57 - 71
Leona MOTORA - Japan	2 - 64 (down)
Elsa PARENT - France	21 - 31 - 38 - 59 - 74
Aurélien PARENT - France	12 - 14 -26 - 51 - 60 - 61 - 62 - 63 - 65 (up)
Dana ROTMAN - Israel	64 (up) - 77 - 90 - 92
Adam ROTMAN - Israel	35 - 68 - 94
Paulina STEINMAYER - Germany	34 - 69 - 73 - 80 - 82
Lily STREETER - USA	36 - 46 - 76 - 78 - 83 - 86
Rong TAN - Singapore	67 - 70 (up)

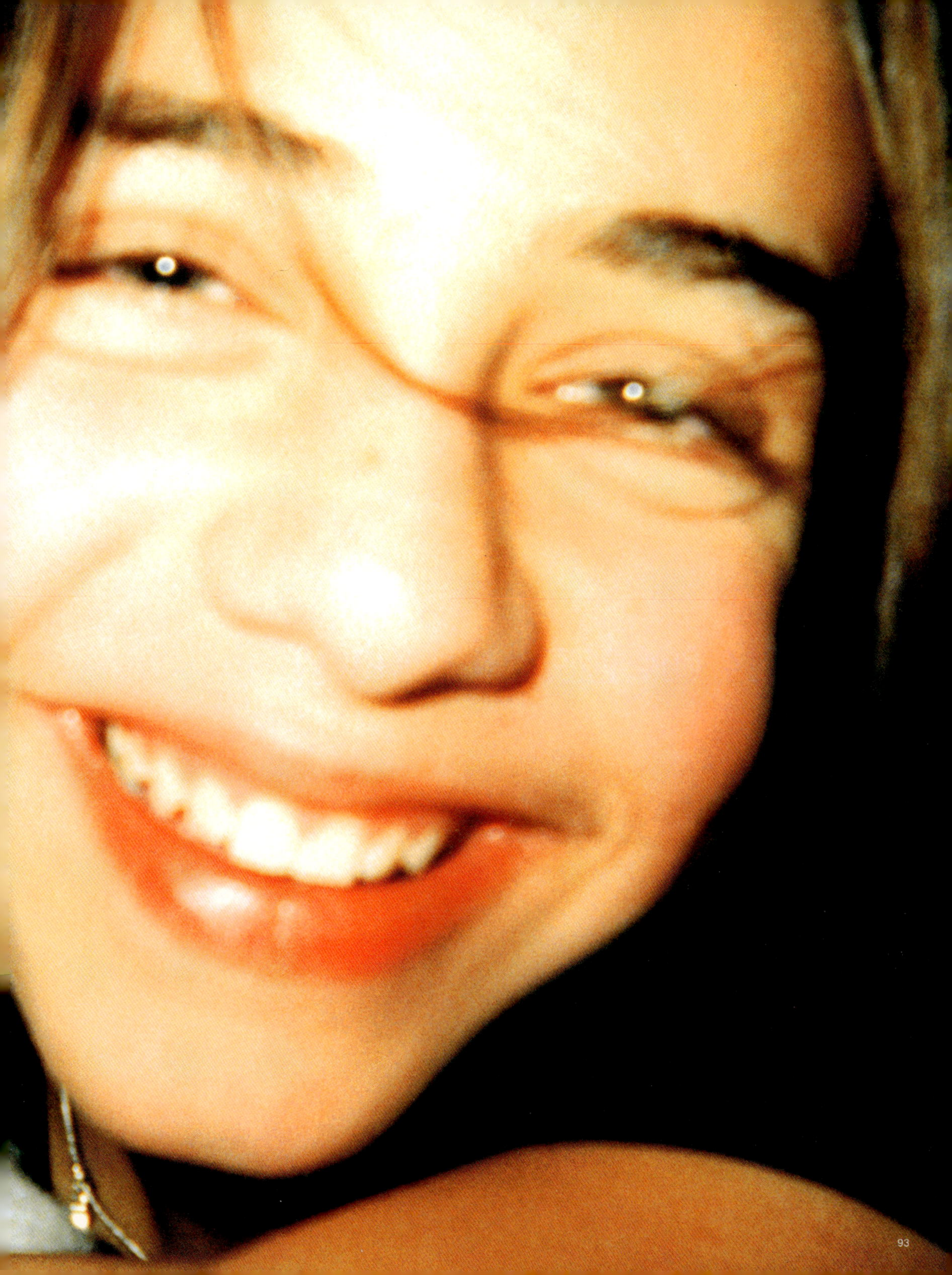

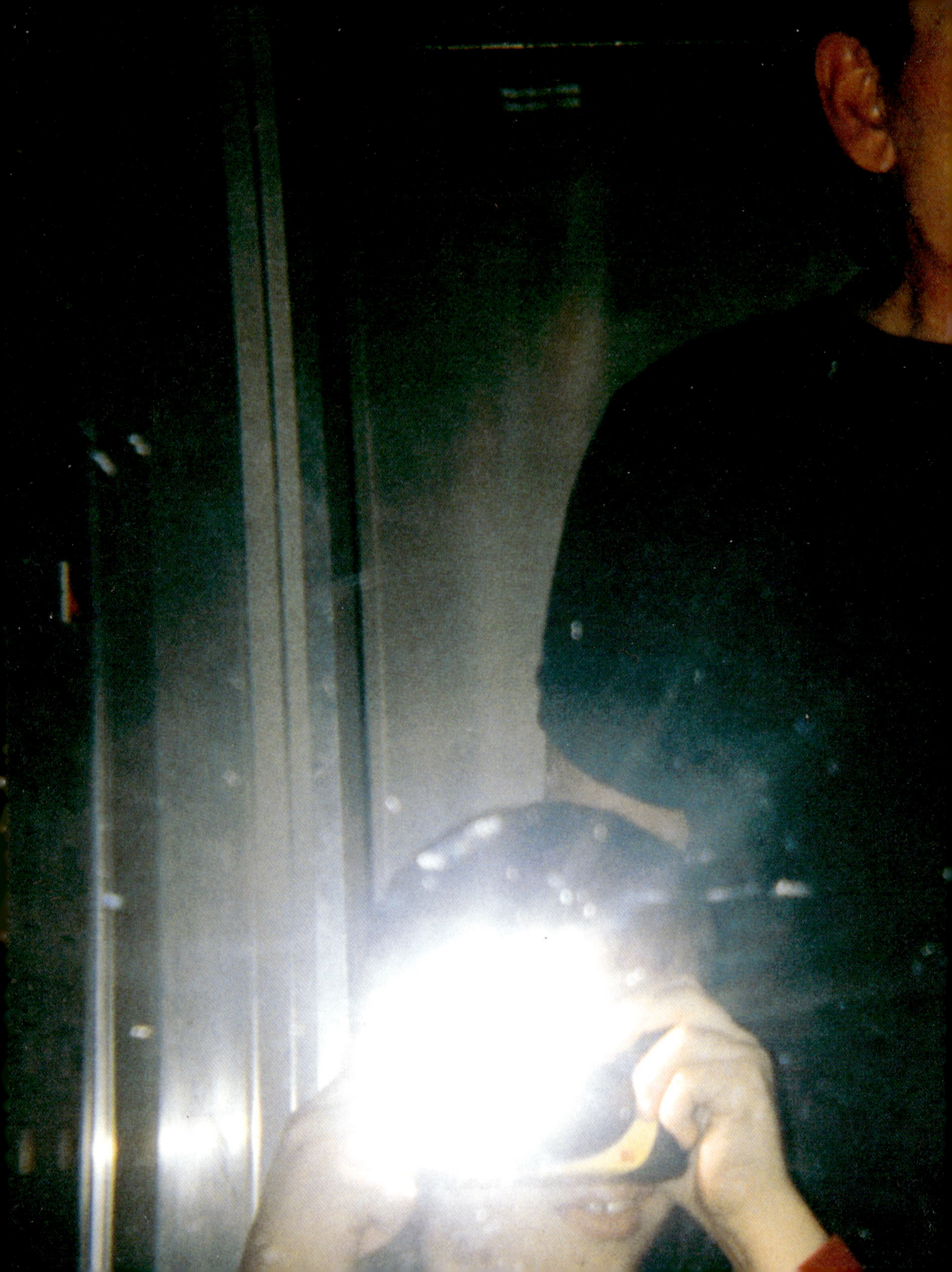